D0481425

# Families and Forgiveness

## Healing Wounds in the
## Intergenerational Family

# Also by Terry D. Hargrave

*FINISHING WELL: AGING AND REPARATION*
*IN THE INTERGENERATIONAL FAMILY*
(coauthored with William T. Anderson)

# Families and Forgiveness

## Healing Wounds in the Intergenerational Family

### Terry D. Hargrave, Ph.D.

BRUNNER/MAZEL *Publishers* • New York

**Library of Congress Cataloging-in-Publication Data**
Hargrave, Terry D.
  Families and forgiveness : healing wounds in the
  intergenerational family / by Terry D. Hargrave
       p.      cm.
  Includes bibliographical references and index.
  ISBN 0-87630-735-7
  1. Forgiveness.  2. Family.  3. Interpersonal communication.
  4. Intergenerational relations.  5. Family psychotherapy.
  I. Title
  BF637.F67H37    1994
  248.8'6—dc20                                      93-43736
                                                         CIP

*Published by*
BRUNNER/MAZEL, INC.
19 Union Square West
New York, New York 10003

Manufactured in the United States of America
10  9  8  7  6  5  4  3  2  1

*To My Loving and Trustworthy Parents,*
*Charley and Janice*

# Contents

# Preface

Families, no matter how damaging they are and appear, also have resources and strengths. I unapologetically carry this belief as one of my fundamental tenets in therapeutic practice. I have seen it in many ways in many different people. A young mother who came from a family where she was raped by her father and then thrown out by her mother seeks to nurture her new husband and baby with responsible tenderness. A husband who was physically abused as a child seeks help whenever he feels himself losing control of his temper to the point where he might become abusive with his own family. A poor and uneducated woman in an abusive relationship works two jobs so her daughter can attend a special private school to get a better education. These are just a few of the many stories that I see every day where people overcome tremendous obstacles with seemingly little going for them.

In reality, however, these people tap into a powerful energy that seems common to humankind: the ability to love and to be trustworthy. Certainly not all people tap the resource. I also see many families and people who are irresponsible and use hate as a daily method of retaliation as they pass destructive tendencies from one generation to the next. Even in these situations, however, I believe the resource and the energy—however meager—are somewhere in the individuals and families.

Nowhere do I see this fundamental belief about family strength more evident than in the work of forgiveness. The very family situations that produced violations of love and trust are turned around to restore and nurture the very heart of what was damaged in the family members. It is in the salvage and restoration effort in the family that I think the resources and the strengths of the group are most evident. I have come to this belief in family strengths not only through what I see in the therapy room; I have seen the resources tapped in my own family. At times when I thought my own family was a lost cause and would fly apart at the seams, it not only survived but came together in a stronger way than I thought possible. It was these powerful changes in therapy and in my own family that started my thinking on the therapeutic value of forgiveness.

Forgiveness is achieved in a variety of situations by many people in many different ways. As I began my work in this area, I found a wealth of religious material and some theories about stages of forgiveness. I also found some therapeutic information that spoke of forgiveness but gave no specifics to people or therapists on the mechanics of the phenomena. So I began to conceptualize a component framework of how forgiveness can occur for individuals and families. It is important to realize that this book is only one conceptualization of the forgiveness process. I do not maintain or expect that it should be the only way people can or should think about the issue. It is simply one method of examining a very complex and heavy therapeutic process that I, and many of my clients and colleagues, have found helpful in the healing, salvage, and restoration of the family after severe violations of love and trust have occurred in the intergenerational family.

I conceptualize the work of forgiveness as four stations: two of exonerating and two of forgiving. In *Section One: "The Four Stations of Forgiveness,"* I outline each station. This section contains the framework of forgiveness, and I believe it is appropriate reading for the therapist and nontherapist alike. Since my thinking about forgiveness has been so heavily influenced by my experience in my own family, I include some of my family story as well as an overview of the work of forgiveness in *Chapter One, "Love, Trust, and Family." Chapter Two, "Station One: Insight,"* includes a discussion of the origins of family pain and the ways that insight can be used to make initial inroads to trustworthiness by stopping and blocking the perpetuation of unjustified actions that cause harm.

Any person who has experienced a severe violation of justice in the family knows the pain caused from guilt and shame. In *Chapter Three, "Station Two: Understanding,"* the origins of guilt and shame are discussed, along with how the second station of understanding can rework perspective on the violation to eventually reduce pain. The tough and risky work of forgiveness is covered in *Chapter Four, "Station Three: Giving the Opportunity for Compensation."* In this chapter, forgiving is discussed as a process by which the victim gives the victimizer the opportunity to demonstrate love and trust in the present context to rework and rethink the family past. Finally, in *Chapter Five, "Station Four: The Overt Act of Forgiveness,"* a step-by-step process is covered on how an overt confrontation between a victim and relational culprit can result in the restoration of love and trust.

In *Section Two, "The Work of Forgiveness in Therapy,"* I try to demonstrate how the four stations play out in a therapeutic situation. Each chapter is a case[*] from my own practice in which I discuss the details of how the client achieved some element of salvage or restoration in the family. In *Chapter Six, "Helping Family Members Forgive One Another,"* I try to give an overview of the therapeutic issues facing the therapist who is helping an individual or family work through tough violations. The goals, pace, and assessment of forgiveness are covered in this chapter, as well as the role the therapist should play in each particular station.

*Chapter Seven, "Clinical Application of Insight,"* discusses the details of a case in which a woman who had been sexually abused in childhood learns through insight to salvage herself and stop the perpetuation of her pain to her children.

In *Chapter Eight, "Clinical Application of Understanding,"* I team up with my colleague William T. Anderson to write about a

---

[*] - All cases have been disguised so that the people involved cannot be identified.

family who deals with the pain of an alcoholic past that continues to be felt in the present. I worked as the therapist in the first part of this case, with Bill as my supervisor. The family re-presented themselves to therapy about two years later, and Bill took on the job of therapist while I had the opportunity to view several sessions from behind a one-way mirror.

Forgiveness is not an issue just in intergenerational families. There are many violations that are experienced in *horizontal relationships*, such as between spouses. *Chapter Nine, "Clinical Application of Giving the Opportunity for Compensation,"* discusses a distressed relationship between a couple where the wife had been betrayed by her husband after she had been faithful to him all their married life. Finally, in *Chapter Ten, "Clinical Application of the Overt Act of Forgiving,"* a woman who had remembered her father sexually abusing her learns how to constructively confront her father with the issue and make their relationship less painful and more constructive.

In *Section Three, "Issues and Questions in the Work of Forgiveness,"* I try to include some answers on common questions that I am asked about the process of forgiveness. I conclude the final chapter with some thoughts about the promise of forgiveness and the potential hope that it offers for humanity as a whole.

If there has been anything that I have learned through working with families dealing with forgiveness, it is that it is difficult work that is hammered out in a process. Although I am sure there are exceptions, most family members do not experience forgiveness as a once-and-for-all event that happens at a place and time, with all issues being resolved completely. Most of us forgive and then go about the process of working out forgiveness as we experience love and trust where we once experienced violation. The four stations of forgiveness are not stages or prescriptions; they are places along the road where most of us wander in our quest to make ourselves and our past whole.

No work such as this is ever accomplished without significant contribution from many people. I want to express my special thanks to the many individuals and families that have demonstrated true commitment and caring in dealing with past pain. They have inspired me by their courage. Also, to my wife, Sharon, I extend my gratitude for her patience and encouragement in moving these ideas out of my personal experience into a therapeutic approach. Finally, I wish to express my love and gratitude to my parents, Charley and Janice. They have been loving teachers on how to restore and redeem brokenness and access the resources that I hardly realized existed in my family. When I rock, cuddle, and love my children in a trustworthy manner, I am thankful for the heritage they have passed along that enables me to give in such a way.

# *Families and Forgiveness*

## *Healing Wounds in the Intergenerational Family*

*Section One*

# The Four Stations of Forgiveness

*Chapter One*

# LOVE, TRUST, AND FAMILY

A s a species, human beings are enormously blessed with the ability to heal physically. But even as tenacious as human life is, we are remarkably vulnerable to injury, disease, and death. Emotionally and relationally, we also have amazing resilience. It is our families that build this resource of resilience by assuring us that they indeed love us and that they can be trusted. Relationships and emotional damage can be held in check if there is a resource of love and trust. No matter how irresponsible the act, how harsh the anger, how hideous the ramifications in the family, relationships survive when people are loved and trusted. On the other hand, in families where the resource of love and trust is depleted, relational and emotional energy drain is almost a foregone conclusion; it does not matter how insignificant the act, how innocent the remark, or how minor the damage.

This book is about forgiveness and how the work of forgiving can reach into the family—any family—and heal the damaged past to the point where a resource of love, justice, and trust can be built. Forgiveness, because it has ramifications for the past and the future of relationships, is a long road of tough work with many potential risks. But accomplishing the work of forgiveness is perhaps one of the supreme manifestations of relationship because it has to involve the work of at least two people willing to trust and rebuild their relationship, even after severe damage.

Perhaps because forgiveness happens in so many different ways and because it is so difficult, there is almost global confusion among families and therapists alike concerning its accomplishment. Many believe forgiveness carries too many indictments of guilt and religious decrees to be useful in therapy. I have found the therapeutic work of forgiveness to be effective not only as an intervention but as powerful vortex where the family past and future can be changed simultaneously.

Like most of the therapy that I use with clients, these ideas of forgiveness have been test driven in my own family. The description of the stations of forgiveness—insight, understanding, giving the opportunity for compensation, and the overt act of forgiveness—includes stories not only of the therapeutic journeys of clients but also of my own journey with my family.

## LOVE AND TRUST IN MY FAMILY

In 1948, in the vast coldness of space and a little past the orbit of the planet Neptune, an almost imperceptible turn of the great comet Halley changed its direction from extension outward from the solar system inward toward its 1985–86 apparition. It was this gentle turn inward that guaranteed that comet Halley would continue to fulfill its promise and tradition to humanity. The turn of this stale dirty snowball only a few miles in diameter directed Halley to its regular fruition when its brilliant coma would be one of the brighter objects in the night sky and its tail would stretch for millions of miles across the solar system. Its fiery torch, which has appeared approximately every 75 years for centuries, has marked the time to generations as they bask in its beauty, remember its history, and even fear its omens.

A little less than a year later, a barely witnessed generational turn took place on the stark plains of New Mexico. This generational turn in my family appeared to be minimal, but it put my intergenerational group on a course where a new apparition of love and trust would appear. In 1949, my parents eloped and married.

Charley Bevard, my father, was the tenth of 12 children. He had grown up in a Depression family that clung to existence after his father lost his arm in a railroad accident. They moved to homestead in New Mexico on some parched land they tried to farm and continued the struggle as the children left home one by one to try to improve their lot in life. Lola Janice, my mother, was the oldest of five children. Her family also homesteaded in New Mexico, but chose ranching as their primary occupation. Like her mother and her grandmother before her, she fought and argued constantly with her mother as she tried to break free of oppressive expectations and find her own place and personality. In an almost flippant manner, she decided to take my father up on his marriage proposal (even though they had had only a few dates) because she could not face telling her father that she had got in trouble at school and had been sent home early. My father, perhaps because he was older, having spent time in the service, or perhaps because he was stricken in love, heartily agreed to the marriage. The same day, they loaded up in a car with a couple of friends to witness the affair and started their lives together. With this very quick and unplanned turn of events, the generational torch was passed along and my parents were set on their family course together.

Along this new course, my parents would have four children in 6½ years. I was the youngest of these four. As one might expect, they struggled hard to maintain existence while they grew up together. When I was four, my mother made the courageous decision to take her high school equivalency exam and start college to become a teacher. My father took two jobs and tenaciously worked my mother through college until she had secured a public teaching position. In turn, my mother worked my father through his degree as a science teacher.

Although my family struggled, we never were hungry and seldom went without things we wanted or needed. But there was something that was desperate in my family that was very difficult for me to describe as a child. My sister fought and argued with my mother in much the same way that my mother struggled with hers; at age 18, my sister eloped to marry a man with whom she had had only a few dates. My oldest brother became alienated from the family, and after several years of tension and threats drifted into the service and marriage. My next brother struggled to fit in and be recognized for his own uniqueness. I experienced tasks as overwhelming and felt incompetent, but it felt safer to keep these feelings to myself. Like much of my family, I labored in loneliness. I grew up—and I suspect that my brothers and sister did also—with the feeling that we were on our own. Family members, siblings included, were not quite to be trusted. Love was scarcely mentioned. The intent of family, as far as I could tell, was to enable you to survive until you were out on your own. There was a family pain that everyone in my household felt, but no one could quite articulate. Something was desperately wrong.

As I articulate it now, I realize my parents were immature, manipulative, relationally unstable, and—regrettably—emotionally and physically abusive. It was not that my parents did everything wrong. Much of their parenting was right on target. But the times that were damaging were such that they left me with the overall impression that I was not loved and my family could not be trusted. Facing these facts and specific incidents was enormously painful for me. They are extremely painful even today.

The abuse for me personally, although there were many times that things were out of control, came to a watershed one evening when I was 8 years old. Looking back, I suppose I was somewhat depressed. I seemed to be unable to have significant contact with anyone in my family, performed poorly in school, and was clearly regarded as incompetent in my neighborhood. I also knew that my parents were struggling to stay above water and not drift into hopelessness. Financially, they were struggling while they were trying to get through college. Physically, they were struggling to keep up with the horrendous work schedule  they had set for themselves, manage a household, and take care of four children. Emotionally, they struggled with each other in a relationship that had already had one lengthy separation and intense fights. My home was not a happy place when I was 8.

Feeling the pain of my own incompetence and carrying the pain of my family's lack of nurture, I made my decision to "end it all." I went into the bathroom and selected one of my father's razor blades and carefully sliced into my forearms. Of course, I knew to avoid cutting my wrists or I would be in serious trouble and might really die! But the slicing of several wounds into both of my forearms was enough to cause quite a mess. The reaction of my family to this attempt was cold, threatening, and uncaring. After discovering what I had done, they left me in the bathroom with no more than threat ringing in my ears. I was left alone. My heart pounded in fear as I felt I had narrowly escaped. A toxic shame coursed through my entire being. Unable to put words to it then, I have come to recognize this awful watershed event as the day I decided for sure that my family did not love me. I felt I had the overt proof they believed they would be better off without me. When I tried to manipulate a declaration of love from them by purposely botching suicide, I received the heinous statement that not only was I not loved, I was not wanted.

This is the root of shame in the family: People who should love you the most and whom you trust with your very life damage you with what appears to be total disregard. For the rest of my years at home, I laid low and never ventured into any activity that would force another family declaration. But the shame and the loneliness remained intact for many years to come.

## COMETS AND FAMILIES

Halley and other comets are members of the solar system, but are very different from anything else that orbits the sun. At one end of its orbit, Halley's comet is small, slow, dead, unwitnessed, and undramatic. But on the other end, the comet is flung to an explosive turn dangerously close to the sun, which animates the woefully small object to dramatic proportions that burn in our memories for a lifetime.   So different are the attributes of the comet at opposite ends of its orbit that it was just a little over two centuries ago that Edmund Halley finally recognized that the periodic appearances of the comet were actually the "returns" of the same object.

This inward and outward journey is what makes us like Halley's comet.  We are bound to our families much in the same way a celestial object is maintained in orbit.  Imperceptible pushes and pulls from family members nudge us toward familiar and repetitious patterns that have been played out for generations in our lineage.  Even when we are the most removed from our family—when we appear alone, dormant, and unanimated—we actually are still on a course that will eventually bring us back into relation with other family members.

As with Halley's comet, it is the journey inward that is uncontrolled, dramatic, and dangerous.  In its tight orbit closest to the sun, the comet struggles against the intense gravitational pull of the gigantic object to maintain its celestial integrity.  What we see as the comet's tail is actually comet "stuff" that has been strewn across space as a witness to the cost of the comet's membership in the solar system.  When we are close to our families, we have a dual potential to experience a beautiful fruition of intimacy or damage from manipulation or abuse.  The journey outward from the family also carries a dual potential.  Away from our families, we are either secure and confident in our delineation of selves as we set out to discover our own limits or on an outward-bound retreat to loneliness.

It is along this journey toward and away from family that we find the basic elements that keep humanity in orbit and in the family.  These elements, stated most simply, are love and trust.  Every question of our existence in the family centers on these two most basic elements.  These are the universal laws that make the family universe work.  If my family does not love me and revel in my being with unconditional positive regard, or if they cannot be trusted and choose to use, abuse, and manipulate me for their own destructive ends, I cannot survive. I will fly off of my orbit and eventually wither and die from neglect and harm. It is in the confines of a family that takes joy in me and that I can trust to seek my best good that I grow and mature. So in the most elemental form, there are two questions we ask of family: *Does my family love me? Is my family trustworthy?*

Most of us answer the question with a qualified yes—qualified because none of our families are perfect. I do not know of one human being who could ever love another in a totally unconditional manner; neither have I known one who never had an impure motive. We all have a tendency to look out for our own consideration before we look out for the other guy. But we extend ourselves to family perhaps more than to others. Parents consistently put the wishes of their children above their own. Many spouses dedicate and commit themselves to each other and go about the endless work of humility and compromise to discover the joy of intimacy with another human who is no blood relation. Most children maintain an intense loyalty to their families, clinging to those relationships as a fruit clings to a life-giving vine. So despite the imperfections in families, most people experience them as places of safety, security, and love that can be counted on when the chips are down.

In families such as these, persons are relatively free to move on the inward and outward journeys in which their orbits take them. Even intense and close inward journeys that produce disagreement or difference are colored with the security that members love and trust one another and will not tear each other apart. Even when individuals are outward-bound on their own and have almost no contact with their families, they go with the confidence of best wishes for success and security and knowledge of a safe haven if things go awry. Relational or emotional hurts between members of these families are like the cuts, bruises, and scrapes that we experienced as children. They hurt—sometimes intensely—and then they heal, leaving no pain and little or no scar.

But some of us will answer the question, Does my family love me and is my family trustworthy? with an unqualified no. This conclusion makes normal family functioning almost impossible.

Sacrifice is sparingly made by spent parents who resent the fact that they receive little or no recognition or compensation for their effort. Spouses move to extremes of either enmeshed relations where one is not allowed to function without the other or boundaries that are so rigid that the two are like alienated roommates. Children are still loyal, but their resilience and resources become drained as they receive the confusing message of love and hate. In these families, looking out for oneself is a necessity for survival. Each inward journey into the family means risk of losing one's emotional self and perhaps experiencing physical harm. Outward journeys often mean cutoffs that offer neither the alleviation of pain nor the confidence of eventual safety. Relational and emotional hurts in these families are quite severe. They leave scars and pain that remain for years. Some injuries may fester and swell for the entire life course and may never heal. Other damage is so profound that relational or even physical life may be in question.

The damage may come in many forms. As S.L. Smith (1991) has outlined, family pain may result from physical mistreatment, emotional mistreatment, neglect, long-standing addictions, or sexual abuse. But the reality that makes this pain of a damaging family so severe is my underlying understanding that my family does not love me and is not trustworthy. The pain of that reality is inescapable. If I try to continue the relationship and move inward, I am usually hurt worse and damaged again. If I move outward or keep my distance, I keep the pain to myself and find it almost impossible to find a safe haven. I am damned if I do and damned if I don't. Without fundamental change in the relationship, the hopeless course seems to be set. These are the situations where the therapeutic intervention of forgiveness is perhaps most powerful.

## THE THERAPEUTIC WORK OF FORGIVENESS

I fancy myself somewhat of a backyard astronomer. I am one of the strange birds that loves to search the stars for faint smudges of light in a telescope eyepiece when most of the world is asleep. The thing that really hooked my interest in astronomy, however, was when I learned as a boy of the future, 1985–86, apparition of Halley's comet.

When the first sighting of Halley was made in deep space in the early 1980s by a huge telescope, my plans were already taking shape to make the most of my once-in-a-lifetime opportunity to view the comet. Because of the distance between Halley and the earth and the alignment that would make the comet be most prominent in the extreme southern sky, it would be the poorest visual apparition of the comet in two millennia. But that did not matter. This was my opportunity and I was going to make the most of it. I constantly read about viewing techniques, photography methods, and the comet's history and characteristics.

As I read, I longed for stories about the comet during the 1910 apparition. Halley put on a spectacular display in 1910, and I found myself wondering what my grandparents' and great grandparents' lives were like back then as they watched the show. This is what caused me to stumble on the idea of putting a time capsule together so people like me in the year 2061—the next apparition—would know how life for my family was in 1986.

At the time, I was stalwart on the idea that I would not have children. It was my destructive way of putting an end to the abuse in my intergenerational family. If family could not be trusted, then I would not expand the family and would deny myself and my parents further offspring. But I felt that someone in the Hargrave family would be around at that time and would be interested.

It was as I began to think about the contents of the time capsule that my anxiety steadily increased. Time capsules tell the future about what life was like when the capsule was put together, and about the people who put their hearts and souls into the effort. My heart and soul were split. There was part of me that was actually okay. I had a wonderful wife who cared for me and some clear direction in life. But the other part was still waning from the burden of incompetence and loneliness. My destructive anger and self-justifying pain would seep out every now and then from behind the strong wall that I had fortified to hold it back. There were times that I was surprised at how angry I got and how close I could come to being downright abusive myself.

So which part was I going to tell the future—only the good parts about myself or the bad parts on how I struggled with my family? I truly did want to be honest with myself, but honesty in this setting would mean that I would have to involve my parents and my intergenerational past. Questions flooded my mind. Could they be trusted? Would they love me enough to even participate? Would they be able to talk to me about the past without using it against me?

In the midst of this struggle, my grandfather on my mother's side was diagnosed with inoperable stomach cancer. The doctors gave him the option of staying in the hospital or going home to die. True to the tough old cowboy he was, he chose to go back to his home in the small town of Roy, New Mexico, where he had been a rancher for most of his life. My wife and I traveled with my mother to visit him for what I knew would be the last time. At the end of our weekend visit, I was at a loss for words. I felt rejection from him. It was not that he was directly physically or emotionally abusive to me, but I could tell that I was not held in high regard with him. Even then, I suspected that my mother had learned the pattern of abuse from her mother and father. His lack of trust was just as profound as that in my family, and it was kept just as quiet.

The time came to say goodbye for the last time. Something was desperately wrong. Although I cannot remember exactly what I said, I stepped up to his bedside saying something inappropriate and inadequate, like "Take care of yourself." After I stepped back, my mother took his hand and said, "Daddy, I will see you next week." No tears were shed between us, and we probably would have parted much in the same way that we always lived—alone, with pretense of intimacy—had it not been for my wife.

Sharon, who knows the severe pain of not being able to say goodbye to loved ones, stepped up to my grandfather's side with tears in her eyes. She took his chubby face into both of her hands and tenderly stared into his eyes and said, "I love you, and I will miss you." These simple words blew the lid off my family's cover. She unknowingly had exposed us for what and who we were. The void of intimacy, love, and trust was exposed. Although my grandfather, my mother, and I scrambled to put the genie back in the bottle, I suppose that we all knew that we could never act quite the same. It was only a few minutes after I left my grandfather's house that I realized that my wife's words were the ones that I wanted to say to him: "I love you, and I will miss you." I did not have the courage. The opportunity to address the issue with my grandfather was lost forever. I walked away, and my mother walked away, in pain that was outside the track of grief.

I suppose that with the passage of time my mother and I could have simulated not having had the issue of love and trust exposed and that we could have gone back to living life as it had always been. But I knew that there would be a day when it was my mother's or father's turn to be on that deathbed. I resolved that when it came that time, I would have this issue of love and trust settled so that I could say to them, "I love you, and I will miss you." So the decision for the time capsule was inescapable. I was going to tell the descendants of the family—the real family. There would be no pretense of intimacy. I would tell the story of the real people and the real family so they could decide who we were for themselves. If it was to be a capsule to the future intergenerational family, then the intergenerational family story would have to be told. For the real story to be told, however, I had to open myself up to the possibility of having a real relationship with my family once again. I would have to be open not only to reviewing the pain of the past but also to living with the possibility of having more pain inflicted on the future.

Why was it so painful? Relationships, and especially family relationships, are unique in their ability to tell us about ourselves. We do not discover that we are loved by nature, and nature certainly does not hold itself to be trustworthy. It is only in relationships in which we discover that we are lovable and safe. When any relationship, but especially one in the family, damages us with some heinous action, the pain is severe. Not only because someone is guilty of irresponsible action that has insulted the balance of justice, but also because we feel shame that we are not lovable and that people who should love us will not put our interests above their own.

When relationships are painful, they are painful because we feel victimized by an irresponsible person who cannot be trusted and shamed because we are not lovable. The *guilt* of a person who has treated us in an unjustified manner strikes hardest at our sense of trust and the *shame* strikes because we realize that we are not loved. It almost goes without saying that the more important the relationship to us, the harder the guilt and shame strike at our being.

This is why forgiveness is necessary in relationships. We want to know that we are loved and that people are trustworthy. Shame, guilt, and fear become overwhelming to us if we believe otherwise. But the task of forgiving takes enormous courage because we may enter back into relationships only to find that people still do not love us and that they still cannot be trusted. However, if we cut ourselves off from our families, we lock in the shame and guilt in such a way they cannot be addressed. How, then, do we help ourselves and others constructively change the past and forgive where it can be changed and move on in other relationships where no change is possible?

The work of forgiveness in families, in my opinion, fits into two broad categories of *exonerating* and *forgiving*. Exonerating and forgiving are both on the same road and neither is inherently better than the other. Exonerating is the effort of a person who has experienced injustice or hurt to lift the load of culpability off the person who caused the hurt (Boszormenyi-Nagy & Krasner, 1986). Instead of subjecting the wrongdoer to endless condemnation, the exonerating person learns how the environment and patterns of the injustice develop and understands and appreciates the wrongdoer's situation, options, effort and limits. It is by gaining *insight* and *understanding* that a person who has experienced a tremendous injustice from another family member is able to go about the work of exoneration.

Forgiving differs from exonerating in that forgiving requires some specific action regarding the responsibility for the injustice that caused the hurt. When a relational injustice occurs in a family, the person who is victimized is hurt and it is reasonable for him or her to hold the wrongdoer responsible for the hurt. Trust in the relationship is at risk. Forgiving involves the victimized person's being given legitimate reason to believe that the wrongdoer accepts responsibility for the injustice and hurt caused, while promising to refrain from further injustice. Forgiveness is accomplished when the victimized person no longer has to hold the wrongdoer responsible for the injustice; the wrongdoer holds himself or herself responsible. The relationship between the two can then be reestablished because trust has been restored. Forgiveness can be accomplished by allowing the wrongdoer to compensate for past injustices by being trustworthy in significant ways in the future, and also by overtly addressing the responsibility of the injustice between the two parties. Forgiveness is accomplished by *giving the opportunity for compensation* and by *the overt act of forgiving*.

The road of forgiveness, therefore, has the two broad divisions of *exonerating* and *forgiving* (Figure 1.1). Exonerating has two stations of *insight* and *understanding*, while forgiving has two stations of *giving the opportunity for compensation* and *the overt act of forgiving*. It is clear that even though exonerating and forgiving are along the same road and are aimed at the work of forgiveness, the two are very different and appropriate in different relationships at different times. Also, even though there are four stations in the work of forgiveness, it should not be interpreted that they are *stages,* such that insight precedes understanding, and so on. The stations of forgiveness are of course intertwined, but it is inappropriate to assume that people move through them sequentially or that they do not oscillate between stations many times in the course of the same relationship. The stations of forgiveness are simply constructs for us to better understand the work of forgiveness.

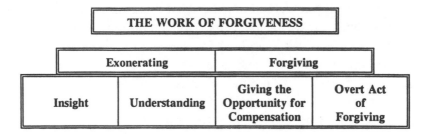

**Figure 1.1** The four stations of forgiveness.

Exonerating and forgiving differ in several ways, but primarily in their demands on the future relationship. Exoneration does not demand responsibility for the injustice, so it does not demand reestablishment of trust. Most often, however, this will limit the type of relationship that two people can have in the future. Exoneration frees a person from the burden of the past hurt or injustice while allowing the person to maintain protection from the relationship that caused the hurt. This is extremely appropriate, especially in relationships that still present risk or where there is an unwillingness from the wrongdoer to accept responsibility.

Forgiveness demands that trust be reestablished between two people after a relational hurt. Essentially, forgiving is relationship reconstruction. For this reason, forgiving puts a person back into a relationship that has caused hurt from injustice in the past. It puts the person in a position of risk in order to build trust. Although forgiving is enormously fruitful, it certainly is not appropriate for every relationship. If I have a parent who was physically abusive when I was small and still threatens me, I would put myself in unwise danger to pursue a forgiving relationship. However, the four stations of forgiveness provide powerful access to alleviating the guilt and shame caused by injustices. Every station represents an effort to come to grips with the relational realities of love and trust in the intergenerational family.

## MY FAMILY OF ORIGIN APPARITION

As I reviewed the pain of my family's past, the anger and hurt over abusive acts, lost memories, uninvolvement, and lack of love began burning in me like a raging fire. But the more the fire raged about the past, the more it met memories of parental sacrifice and care that served as fire walls to the anger. There were two sides to the story much in the same way that there were two divisions in my heart and soul. Halley's comet was coming and I had made a decision about including my past—and my parents—in what I would pass along to the next generation.

Painfully, I came to the point where I was able to issue a half-hearted invitation to my parents to join me in my trip to view the comet and take part in putting together the time capsule for their descendants. To my surprise, they enthusiastically accepted. This encouraged me to invite my parents in for a second look at the past in a constructive manner. Again to my surprise, they were not only willing to talk about the past, but willing to acknowledge responsibility.

In our conversation, they confirmed the abuse in my family, but then went on to tell me the story of their own pain. My father told me about the pain he felt when he and my mother separated when we were children. He told me the stories of his depression after being stationed in Greenland with the Air Force. While he was there, a litany of horrible events occurred: Men froze to death trying to get back to the barracks after using the toilet; he spent 10 straight days in a sleeping bag buried in the snow in sixty-below weather while his group waited for a break in a blizzard; it was an agonizing separation from my mother, with only two items of mail allowed during a yearlong stay. He found out about the birth of my second brother three months after his actual arrival. He spoke of his pain growing up in a large family where there was a lack of love and a profound lack of security.

My mother told me about the regrettable acts of abuse in her own family. She told me about her struggles as she tried to grow up while dealing with her own legacy of shame and guilt. She told me about her mother and her mother's mother and how she believed she learned this lack of care and nurture from them. She said, "I just never realized how important it was to hold and love children. I didn't know you were supposed to rock and cuddle babies. It simply did not occur to me that security given by touch was important." I parked my mother's words in my mind and for the first time in my life I began to understand why she had always defended her parenting skills, saying that she was a good parent. Considering their backgrounds and compared with their parents, my parents had indeed done better.

As I talked with them, they became less powerful and more vulnerable. In response, I became less defensive and it became easier—even enjoyable—to recount the efforts of love and nurture that they had made during my childhood. Issues of the past were certainly not erased, but love and trust in our relationship had shifted it significantly. The more I understood, the more I trusted them. The relationship was changing. After one of these discussions with my parents, I drove outside the city limits and with my telescope I caught my first glimpse of Halley's comet. This time, the sighting was with my own eyes and was not some secondhand report. I had the proof that the great comet was returning.

A few months later, my wife and I, along with our parents, traveled to the Davis Mountains in Texas to view Halley during the peak observation window. During the two nights of observation, I had planned several ritualistic activities. We opened a bottle of wine and toasted our unborn descendants as we recorded what was said. While watching the comet, we read a passage from the Bible declaring the handiwork of God. We made predictions about the future, composed lyrics about the comet, and took pictures of ourselves. The more rituals we performed, the more I realized that I was discovering a unified heart and soul. I no longer felt like two people with a past and a present; love and trust were becoming unified across my life span.

The capsule gave my parents the essential opportunity to express love and trustworthiness to descendants yet unborn. When they expressed the love with their newfound resources, they used me as the medium. The past was not obliterated, but the capsule began to represent a promise of childhood; a contract between my parents and myself that no matter what happened in the past or what would happen in the future, we loved one another and we could be trusted.

At 4:00 a.m., out in the desert mountains, I joined with my parents. The great comet Halley was extremely low in the south-southeast, dimmed by the haze of the horizon and the tremendous distance between it and the earth. It was, by all accounts, the poorest apparition in almost two millleneum. But it was there. Its gentle tail stretched upward across the constellation Scorpio, silhouetted against the background of the Milky Way. My family's beginning of love and trust was not a burst of light of automatic reconciliation, but the clear bond between us secured the intergenerational transition. No matter how unimpressive our first moves toward one another, a new relationship had begun between me and my parents.

Within months, my pain and anger had disappeared. Even with the knowledge of the family past, *the pain and anger were gone*. For the first time in my life, I began to want children. I desired to pass myself and my parents along to *my* offspring. Since the apparition of Halley's comet, there has been a steady growth of love and trust between me and my parents. Not all has been rosy, but there is a security and a continual effort to build the future of the family away from the past injustices and pain.

In 1991, my mother and father went on a mission trip to Brazil with their Presbyterian church group. After two weeks, part of the mission group returned and some others, including my parents, stayed to do some touring. One of the returning members of the mission team reported that my mother was such a loving and caring woman. I must admit, even with the tremendous work that my mother had done through the years at becoming nurturing, my first response was to think, "My mother?" But then came the story.

My mother had taken on as her mission the very young children who were quarantined in the hospital with tuberculosis. For six months, these children would be separated from the care and nurturing of their families. My mother, as reported by the mission team, would sit for six hours a day rocking, holding, and singing to those needy children. My mother knows how important it is to impart love, security, and trust to children. She always did, it was just that now she was able to access the resources she had to give away. And as she rocked those children in Brazil, she was saying to me in a very real way, "If I could do it over again, I would do this for you." And when my mother now holds, rocks, and sings to my children—and holds me as she does—she empowers me and my whole intergenerational family with love and trust.

There is a wooden box containing a time capsule that sits on my bookcase. The following words are inscribed on a brass plaque:

> *To the south-southeast, ours in Winter wanes*
> *Capricornus, Sagittarius, Scorpio and on.*
> *But to the north-northwest, yours in Summer soars*
> *The reed of time, to recount and recall.*
> *Hail Halley! Our generation mark!*

The issue of love and trust is settled for me because of the powerful healing work of forgiveness. My exonerating and forgiving through the various stations of forgiveness has reestablished a broken relationship between me and my parents. When it comes time for my parents to die, I will take their hands, look them straight in the eyes and tell them, "I love you, and I will miss you." My belief is also, that in 2061 when my descendants open the time capsule under the blaze of the comet Halley, the apparition of love and trust will be even stronger and they will be able to say the same to one another.

*Chapter Two*

# STATION ONE: INSIGHT

T he work of forgiveness in families is the work of reestablishing love and trust in relationships. In my relationship with my parents, the most basic elements of love and trust were now different. My internal computer hardware had not changed—I was the same person—but the programmed software of my beliefs and emotions had been updated in an astonishing manner. The interchange between me and my parents had a complex effect on the variables of our past together as a family. So different were my beliefs and feelings about my parents and our pasts that it almost felt magical how the reprogramming occurred. Partially because the work of forgiveness is so complex and partially because it can make such a difference in the emotional reality of the family, many mistakenly think that forgiveness is either unattainable or an almost mystic solution to profound injustices. However, the work of forgiveness is neither too complex nor mystical. The road of forgiveness is difficult, but there are points of demarcation that make the way to proceed clearer. The effects of forgiveness on present relationships may be so significant that it seems like an illusion, but the effects and the relationships are indeed real.

The first point of demarcation in making the road of forgiveness clearer is the station of *insight*. Insight is a method of exonerating that allows people to take initial steps toward trust. When I was younger, I participated in Boy Scouts and learned basic first aid and lifesaving skills. Among the skills and techniques I learned were steps to take in order of priority to help the injured. Even before the most severe wound was treated, the first priority was to try to minimize the risk of further injury by removing the danger. In family relationships, minimizing risk of further relational injury is also the necessary first step. Insight allows persons to see the mechanisms that have caused the damage and hurt, and this perspective then provides them with the means to protect themselves from further hurt and damage.

## FAMILY PAIN AND HURT

Family pain and hurt originate from such a wide variety of sources that it is sometimes difficult for people and therapists to decipher where the relational damage has occurred. The theoretical constructs of contextual therapy (e.g., Boszormenyi-Nagy & Spark, 1984; Boszormenyi-Nagy & Ulrich, 1981; Boszormenyi-Nagy & Krasner, 1986) have been particularly helpful to me in conceptualizing how relational damage originates and how it affects the family.

### Dimensions of Family Relationships

Contextual therapy is a comprehensive family therapy approach that integrates many different premises from several theories of family and psychology. The foundation of the contextual therapy framework is the healing of human relationships through commitment and trust (Boszormenyi-Nagy & Spark, 1984). All relationships exist in four dimensions. Although these four dimensions can be discussed separately, they are intertwined and inseparable in terms of their effect on the family (Boszormenyi-Nagy & Krasner, 1986).

*Facts.* Facts are anchored in existing environmental, relational, and individual factors that are objectifiable. They include factors such as genetic input, physical health, basic historical facts, and events in a person's life cycle.

*Individual Psychology.* The individual's psychology is the subjective internal psychological integration of his or her experiences and motivations. Individual psychology produces subjective influences on relationships as individuals strive for recognition, love, power, and pleasure and are motivated by aggression, mastery, or ambivalence.

*Family or Systemic Transactions.* Family or systemic transactions are the communication or interaction patterns of relationships. The objectifiable transactions produce organization or laws that define power alignments, structure, and belief systems.

*Relational Ethics.* Relational ethics deals with the subjective balance of justice, trustworthiness, loyalty, merit, and entitlement between members of a relationship. As members of the relationship interact in an interdependent fashion, relational ethics require them to assume responsibility for consequences and strive for fairness and equity in the process of give-and-take.

Although each of these dimensions affects relationships, Boszormenyi-Nagy and Krasner (1986) maintain that it is the dimension of relational ethics that is the most powerful and potentially the most therapeutic in the family. Relational ethics is rooted in the philosophical beliefs of Buber (1970), who maintained that individuals are dependent on relationships in order to experience self-understanding and self-delineation. It was also Buber who put forth the idea that humans have an innate sense of justice with which to try to balance what they are entitled to receive from relationships and what they are obligated to give in order to maintain relational existence. When relationships are cast into this relational ethics context, we can understand the function of human emotions. Emotions are simple barometers or gauges that give us a reading on the balance between give and take in relationships. When we do not receive what we deserve, we become angry. On the other hand, when we overbenefit from a relationship we have not contributed to, we may feel guilty. Therefore, the dimension of relational ethics encompasses the emotional field of the individual and family relationships.

When people engage in relationships that have a balanced give-and-take between relational entitlements and obligations, this innate sense of justice is satisfied. Balance between give and take over a period of time produces a sense of trustworthiness in the relationship. At its basic foundation, a trusting relationship provides security that individuals will receive what they deserve in the relationship without having to threaten, manipulate, or retaliate and the freedom to contribute and give in the relationship without fear or apprehension. Trustworthiness is the key resource that enables family members to give to each other, and it therefore provides relational security and stability (Boszormenyi-Nagy & Krasner, 1980).

A few years ago when I was finishing my degree and working on my dissertation, the burden of household duties and the bulk of emotional responsibility fell to my wife. While I strained to take comprehensive exams and collect data, my wife provided almost all the care for our daughter, kept us financially afloat, and was a patient encourager to me. My contribution to the function of our home and my family was minimal. Certainly the relationship was not balanced, and her innate sense of justice was not satisfied. However, my wife extended herself with almost total confidence. The reservoir of trust that we had built into our marriage up to that point allowed her to maintain the freedom of giving to the relationship even though her entitlement was neglected. The reservoir allowed her to have confidence that the situation was temporary and to believe that, if our positions were reversed, I would do the same for her. But even as trusting as my wife was in our relationship, if I had continued to be irresponsible to the relationship for a long period of time, the reservoir of trust would eventually have been depleted. Even the strongest of relationships have their limits if trust is continually being depleted. So even though a relationship need not be balanced between give and take all the time in order to provide a stable and secure environment, imbalance depletes resources of trust and will eventually affect even the strongest relationships.

## Destructive Entitlement

When there is a consistent or severe imbalance in this relational give-and-take, individuals feel that they either have been cheated by or have overbenefitted from relationships. Instead of there being a balance that builds trustworthiness in a relationship, trust is drained and the members of the relationship feel that their just entitlement is threatened. Instead of providing individuals freedom to give and security to receive, the relationship becomes an unstable arena with a dog-eat-dog quality, where individuals strive only to secure their own entitlement. It is again the innate sense of justice that sets individuals in the relationship on this self-justifying claim toward securing compensation for their just entitlement. Boszormenyi-Nagy and Krasner (1986) refer to this violent pursuit of one's entitlement as *destructive entitlement.*

Destructive entitlement can manifest itself in many ways, including paranoid attitudes, hostility, rage, emotional cutoffs, and destructive harm to other individuals. Imbalances in the relational give-and-take and resulting destructive entitlement may be the result of gradual decline in trust or a single violent and destructive act. Gradual declines in trust may result from a number of problems such as emotional barriers, constant manipulation, emotional distance, and irresponsible behavior. Violent and destructive acts deteriorate relationships rapidly because they insult the balance of give-and-take. Most often, these severe acts are intertwined with behaviors that are associated with gradual declines in trustworthiness. Some examples of violent and destructive acts are retribution or intentional manipulation such as frequent verbal attacks or threats; physical harm such as acts of abuse and incest; or irresponsible emotional mistreatment that results from activities such as neglect or addiction.

It is this destructive entitlement that is at the very root of family pain and hurt. The justice and trust that are so necessary for a balanced relational ethic are violated, and family victims of the destructive behavior are left to draw painful conclusions: The people they must depend on the most in the world cannot be trusted. These destructive family members are more interested in their own well-being than in that of their families. This violation of justice and trust in the relational ethics dimension in turn colors every aspect of the other three dimensions.

Resources in the dimension of facts are squandered in damaged families. Because of the family relational emptiness, no amount of money, size of house, change of geographic location, advancement in career, or modification in marital status can release a person from the emotional turmoil caused by lack of trust in one's family. In families where there is severe damage in the relational ethics dimension, factual concerns are blamed (e.g., "My family was spoiled by too much money"), manipulated ("Our relationship will be better if we have a boat to spend time together on the lake"), or exploited ("I cannot be held responsible for my behavior because my people have been abused by society"). Realities in the factual dimension are used to blame, manipulate, and exploit the imbalance in the relational ethics dimension in a particularly destructive way. This was the case with a woman whose children accused her of neglecting them both physically and emotionally when they were younger.

> I grew up in the Depression where you didn't have time for anything but worrying about what you were going to eat. It made me grow up fast and take care of myself. I've been working since I was seven. It made me hard and strong and that's how I raised my children.

The family or systemic interaction dimension is also greatly affected by the destructive imbalance in the relational ethics dimension. Since destructive entitlement is one's self-justifying claim to entitlement at the expense of an innocent party, it is extremely dependent on family organization and power. Therefore, family rules or laws and hierarchy become ingrained dysfunctional patterns as the family struggles to maintain existence amidst relational insecurity. For instance, a child may be hesitant to confront a father's destructive alcohol addiction because of fear of an emotional cutoff or of the parent's throwing himself into a self-defeating drinking binge. Another example of these strong family laws is reported by an adult who refused to deal with incest because of the fear that if the secret were revealed, she would be ostracized by the rest of the family.

> If I speak out against my father, none of them [the siblings] will support me. None of us have ever talked about it openly, and we all act like it never happened. It has screwed up our lives. They will get angry with me for upsetting Mom and Dad and our family times. Dad will deny it.

Family interactions are used to maintain a powerful structure to preserve the family despite the severe damage in the dimension of relational ethics. Double binds, family secrets, domination, and cutoffs are just a few of the interactional patterns and tactics used to deal with destructive entitlement. In the above example, the dysfunctional family structure was held intact by the covert threat of being put out of the family and by the power of the father to deny the truth.

The most powerful effect of this destructive entitlement in the relational ethics realm, however, is on the dimension of individual psychology. As individuals come to the painful realization that the family members who are obligated to care for them cannot be trusted, they internalize the emotional trauma. Most often, individuals will interpret the violation of justice and trust as personal deficiencies, which result in internal shame.  If the violation is severe, therefore, the victim in the family is likely to internalize the experience of being unloved and perhaps, unlovable.  This subjective internalization of being unloved by one's family is an intolerable blow to one's self-concept and image.  This is illustrated by a middle-aged man who recalled the abuse he experienced as a young boy.

> I recall one time after a beating. . . (*long pause*) I realized that my mother did not want me.  (*starting to cry*)  No matter who I was or what I did, she never wanted me or loved me.

Individual responses to shame may vary on a personality continuum from personalities that are perfectionistic and disengaged on one extreme to those that are chaotic and enmeshed on the other, but both are psychological defenses to deal with the painful shame of feeling unloved by family.

Thus pain and hurt in the family originate in the relational ethics dimension because of a continual imbalance in the relational give-and-take.  This imbalance drains trustworthiness from the family, and individual members feel justified in seeking their just entitlement through destructive channels.  This destructive entitlement results in manipulation, dysfunctional family patterns, and, in the worst cases, damage to the psyche of family members who feel the shame of not being loved.

Pain and hurt are very clear in extreme cases where there is overt physical abuse, incest, or profound neglect. However, pain and hurt can be just as real from less extreme acts of destructive entitlement. Consistent lack of interest, manipulation, addictions to drugs and alcohol, may produce tremendous pain and hurt in the family even though the destructive patterns may appear to be less violent. The key component of the pain and hurt is not the actual pattern or destructive act, but the drain of the trust resources in the family. Any act that consistently contributes to the deterioration of family trust will eventually result in family pain and hurt.

Certainly family pain can be caused by factors outside relationships. Genetic accidents, incurable diseases, tornadoes, or earthquakes are just a few examples of how nature can deal a family severe injury. Systems can also do a family harm. A government or race of people may deal harshly with individuals based on the color of their skin or their cultural background. But as Smedes (1984) points out, it is only people who can be held accountable in relationships for the pain and hurt and who can give and accept forgiveness.

Even though pain and hurt originate from the same source—deterioration of trustworthiness—they vary in magnitude. A victim of manipulation from an alcoholic family member and a victim of severe physical abuse will both not trust their families, but the victim of the physical abuse may feel more pain because of the violent act. Generally, family pain accumulates more and more as the severity and longevity of the destructive act increase.

In this framework forgiveness is necessary: When the justified balance of give-and-take is violated to the point where trust in the relationship has evaporated, the resulting damage permeates every aspect of the victimizer's and victim's future relationships. Being unable to trust another to be attentive to their needs, both victimizer and victim have the potential to approach relationships in a defensive or destructive manner to assure self-protection. Internalized guilt and shame over the destructive behavior on the part of both the wronged and the wrongdoer puts self-image and self-esteem in jeopardy. The four stations of forgiveness are aimed at healing this guilt and shame by restoring the justice and trust needed in relationships.

## INSIGHT

Insight, the first station of forgiveness, allows a person to objectify the mechanisms of family pain that have caused the relational damage. Once these mechanisms have been identified, an individual can stop the relational damage from occurring in the future. In this manner, trust is not restored to a relationship between a victim and victimizer, but minimum drain on the remaining trust resources in the relationship is accomplished. Therefore, insight has limited ability to *heal* relationships, but it does put the brakes on additional damage.

Once a person has been a victim of an undeserved hurt, the pain can result in powerful and long-term emotions of guilt, anger, depression, and rage. Because the person is unjustly denied entitlement, he or she has the potential to utilize the same destructive entitlement to secure emotional resources from an innocent party. For example, if I feel unloved because my parents never expressed love to me and expected me to provide security for them, I may feel justified in manipulating my children and holding them responsible for providing love and security for me. We all find ourselves repeating harmful actions or words that we once considered damaging. This revolving slate of injustices (Boszormenyi-Nagy & Spark, 1984) is the family dynamic of imbalances in relational ethics. The victim, because of the innate sense of justice and rightful claim to entitlement, is always at risk to become a victimizer. In this way, the beat goes on and family damage and the resulting pain are perpetuated. This is seen in the following statement from a father in his mid-thirties who was accused of physical abuse.

> I'm tired of all this. It is time they [the children] start respecting who I am. It's always been the same crap. I had to take crap from my family all my life when they didn't give a rip about me. I deserve a little peace from my children. I'll treat them the way I see fit!

Insight works in two directions. First, for the victim, insight clarifies the relational issues such as who is responsible for the damage, the transactions that perpetuate the destructive behavior, and the internalized implications of love and trust. Second, for the potential victimizer, insight provides a method to check one's behavior to ensure that one is not inflicting the same type of damage on an innocent party that was once inflicted on oneself. In short, insight helps me protect myself from future manipulation and damage and protect others from my own potential for retaliation and retribution.

## Insight and the Dimension of Relational Ethics

My dog once killed a squirrel out in our backyard and, without our knowledge, deposited the carcass in the bushes beside our kitchen door. Each time my wife and I went into our kitchen, we were increasingly aware that something was wrong. The fault was not our senses—we could smell the problem. The fault lay with our inability to locate the source of the problem. No matter how much we avoided the kitchen, no matter how we scowled, the odor remained. It was not until we stumbled across the unfortunate animal outside that we were able to extricate its awful effects from our house. When we experience severe relational injustices, our emotions clearly tell us something is wrong. We feel used, abused, manipulated, and cheated. But these feelings do not necessarily direct us to the real problem. Insight into the dimension of relational ethics is necessary for a person to pinpoint the source of injustice.

The primary requirement in order to gain insight into the dimension of relational ethics is to track down the reasons for the emotional status of the damaged relationship. Violation of justice means that we feel unloved and believe the relationship to be untrustworthy. The violation must be identified. This may sound easy enough, but when we are dealing with family members with whom we have long histories and who have hurt us unjustly, it can become confusing. Because of the pain, we often have trouble articulating exactly what the violation of trust was and the indication that we were not loved. This is seen in the story told by an adult daughter whose father had several affairs and then finally deserted the family when she was a teenager.

I really don't care what went on between him and my
mother. What I hate him for is that when we would go see
him, he would never ask about us [the children]. He was
only interested in himself and what he was doing. I can't
remember once that he ever asked about me and my life
after he left.

There is little doubt that this daughter was expressing true pain
and a sense of violation in the fact that her father did not take an
interest in her, but the original source of the pain is unclear. The
fact that her father ignored her in subsequent years after leaving
is an interaction that is identifiable, but is it the source of pain that
would cause such hate? It is doubtful that the father's indifference
to the daughter or even the father's desertion is the root of the
violation the daughter feels. More likely is that the daughter
knows that the father consistently put his own entitlement ahead
of his giving to his family. No matter the change in interaction—
whether the father had remained with his family or even if he had
taken an interest in his daughter—the pain from destructive neglect
would have likely remained.

Insight into this dimension relies on the ability of a person to
identify the source of relational imbalance in the give-and-take in
the relationship and thereby identify the real source of emotional
pain. Most often, this realization will not be specific destructive
action on the part of the victimizer, but instead will focus on the
global issue of balance and trust in the relationship (e.g., "My
father could not be trusted," "He put his interests above my own,"
or "He did not give me what I deserved").

Individual emotional reactions to violation from families are
powerful. However, the emotional status of relationships is quite
subjective and difficult to objectify. Because it is subjective,
global, and at times unclear, some victims of relational violation
begin to question the reality of the imbalance or tend to exaggerate
interactions to make the imbalance objective or clearer. For
instance, the following account is from a woman who was sexually

violated by her father, but denied the abuse because it was incongruent with the security needs he provided for her.

> I don't know how to describe it. He made me undress in front of him and interrogated me in detail about my dates. He would accuse me of being loose and say horrible things to me after I would go out. I'm not sure I can say he abused me. Maybe I'm making a bigger deal out of it than it really was.

Our society unreasonably tends to expect individuals to have identifiable proof of the cause of their emotions in order for the emotions to be considered valid. However, the balance in the dimension of relational ethics may not be clearly identifiable in actions, even though the reality of the relational dimension is clear. Many violated individuals may feel the necessity to exaggerate actions in order to "justify" their emotional claims of violation. These exaggerated claims cloud the ability of the individual to gain insight into the relational violation. Such is the case with a woman who was physically abused as a young girl in her family.

> There has never been one person in my life who has ever done one thing for me. Family, children, husband, friends—every one of them has used me.

Insight in the relational ethics dimension allows an individual to clarify the emotional damage that has been caused by being victimized by an injustice. The claim does not have to be justified or proved, nor should it be dismissed or denied. This insight in turn provides the victim with the perspective of knowing where the powerful emotions he or she feels originate. Confidence is secured in knowing exactly where the problem is, that there actually is a problem, and that evidence does not have to be provided to prove the violation. Insight validates the person's feeling of hate, anger, depression, and so on, because it correctly identifies the imbalance in the relational ethic. When victims gain such insight, they identify the specifics of their hurt and the extent of the damage.

This insight also provides the victim with the ability to place the violation and the corresponding emotions with the person who was responsible for the violation. If I was locked in a closet for days at a time for punishment when I was young, I am likely to be untrusting, fearful, or enraged. If, however, I do not have the insight to place the responsibility with the one who violated me, I am likely to be untrusting, fearful, or enraged with anyone with whom I am in relation, including spouse, children, friends, or employers. Insight assists the victim in directing the emotional field to where it belongs, where it does not seep into and poison the emotional status of other relationships.

### Insight and the Dimensions of Family Transactions

Classic family systems theory maintains that families function to maintain homeostasis in order to secure family integrity. In other words, actions in the family are designed to maintain an oscillating "normal" range of how a particular family works. Interactions in the family produce an organization with hierarchy, structure, and beliefs.

Some families develop dysfunctional interactions in order to maintain system integrity. In many of these dysfunctional families, family members repeatedly inflict relational damage on other family members. For instance, two spouses may not be able to tolerate the emotional closeness of an intimate relationship. Arguments, separations, or even affairs may be actions in the system that allow the couple to stay emotionally distant, even though they have little intention of divorcing. The problem is that the action chosen to maintain distance does tremendous relational damage.

When individuals are damaged or violated in an unjust manner in their families, transactions often serve to perpetuate the hurt. In the case of an incestuous family, for instance, the power hierarchy of the family will often not allow a violated child to overtly confront the abusing parent. Beliefs about loyalty or respect, or even fears concerning parents, may result in damaging secrets or rules about behavior. Therefore, the abusing parent may feel the power to say or do sexually inappropriate things, and the family structure and belief system may be such that the behavior has to be tolerated. *The organization of the family that allowed the damaging transaction to occur in the first place will allow the damage to occur in the future.* In this way, family transactions often perpetuate the pain of a victim even though no future violation may occur. The individual rightfully feels at risk in a system where he or she has been hurt before and where nothing has changed.

Since family and systemic transactions are objectifiable, insight into this dimension can be most helpful. The identification of patterns, communication, and family rules gives the person who has been hurt unjustly in a family the ability to avoid or stop harmful or painful patterns and break rules that perpetuate damaging interactions. For instance, an adult daughter who had been sexually abused by her father reported that she had always been heavily involved in her parents' marital relationship. She stated that her mother and father kept secrets from one another, but would tell their secrets to her and she would then be expected to hold their confidences.

The woman continued to be triangulated into her parents' relationship even though she had long since left their household and had an apartment of her own. She hated to hear from either of her parents, and she reported violent anger toward both her mother and her father concerning her victimization by her father. When the therapist pointed out the triangulation of the daughter into the parents' relationship and suggested that she stop carrying intimate secrets for them, the woman quickly came up with a solution, which she reported on the next visit.

> I decided to keep a running list of what each one told me.
> At the end of the week, I sent each of them a copy of what
> the other one had said. My mom called and asked me why
> I did such a thing and I told her that it was just my way of
> helping them out and that I was planning to do it in the
> future. Needless to say, neither of them has said a word
> about the other to me this week. I can feel the tenseness,
> but I'm going to force myself not to get involved.

Although the woman's actions caused extreme discomfort for
her parents, the change in family transaction put the marital
intimacy where it belonged. The daughter still suffered from the
pain of the incestuous violation, but she had developed a transactional intervention that protected her from future injustice.

Insight into the dimension of family and systemic transactions
often provides victims of family injustice the ability to recognize
the mechanisms that aggravate and perpetuate their emotional
pain. This in turn often is helpful to them in recognizing their own
patterns of destructive or retaliatory action. Generally, the better
a person is able to articulate how dysfunctional family patterns
contributed to his or her pain, the better that person will be able
to guard against repeating such patterns in other relationships.
Simply stated, insight in this dimension helps people recognize
family actions and situations that "hook" them so they can avoid
the hook in the future.

### Insight and the Dimension of Individual Psychology

We all learn about who and what we are in the framework of
relationships. Even our genetic makeup is an unknown to us until
we try it out within the context of our family and environment. In
the midst of these interactions, we internalize certain beliefs about
what is true about our personhood and how others perceive us.

As mentioned before, individuals who have been the victim of
an unjust relational balance between give and take are at risk.
Their families are unjust and untrustworthy; therefore, they may

assume that they are unworthy of entitlement and unlovable in relationships. No matter what family violation occurs, victims usually internalize the pain at some level to a "belief" about themselves.

Insight into the dimension of individual psychology is perhaps the most difficult to gain. The mechanisms by which one learns about oneself are as secure as what one expects to see in the mirror upon getting up in the morning. Beliefs about oneself are not just habits—they are the core of our familiarity. Change in one's internal psyche is of course possible, but is difficult with insight alone. Since we originally learn about ourselves in the context of family relationships, it is often those very family relationships that are necessary to modify those beliefs.

Insight, however, is not void of power in this dimension. Western societies have always placed large stock in the worth and value of the individual. We have emphasized this perspective in our culture, government, and expression. However, even in societies that are more oriented toward the value of the group, there is the belief that each individual makes a valued contribution to the whole. Human beings are complex and wonderfully constructed in both thought and action. Insight does provide a basic understanding that all individuals have value and worth just by virtue of their humanness.

Insight also offers individuals the ability to understand the forces that shaped their personalities. If I was never allowed to explore my environment when I was a toddler and was corrected and scolded every time I tried something new, I may well have internalized feelings of self-doubt, about which I can gain insight. In the same vein, insight can provide me with the ability to recognize internal conflicts and the means by which I seek to resolve those conflicts in present relationships. Such was the case with an older woman who was separated from her husband.

> My father was a hard man who never showed much feeling. I wanted him to love me so bad, I would have done just about anything. I tried to be beautiful, work hard, and

be popular. Nothing seemed to work. It's funny—I
married a man who didn't show any feeling either. I guess
I wanted to prove to myself that a person like my father
could love me.

In family relationships where violations of trust have occurred,
people internalize harmful, destructive, and self-defeating messages about themselves. Insight into oneself raises the conscious-
ness of the internal forces that shape personality. Insight into these
issues has the potential of disengaging these forces and allowing
individuals to make different belief choices about themselves. But
more importantly, it allows individuals to recognize how damage
in their pasts has influenced internal motivations toward other
relationships. This permits individuals to make insightful decisions regarding how they use relationships to satisfy strivings for
recognition, love, power, and pleasure.

### Insight in the Dimension of Facts

The dimension of facts includes objectifiable factors such as our
genetic makeup, physical health, gender, cultural heritage, geographic location, and socioeconomic group. Many of us believe
that if the facts of our lives can be manipulated or changed in some
way, we will be okay. For instance, I would be happier or more
satisfied with life if I had a nicer house or car. If I had a better job,
life would be better. There is little doubt that facts do greatly affect
our station in and outlook on life, but the impact of changing facts
on improving relationships is probably overemphasized.

Control over the factual dimension is extremely unstable. We
can work hard, be conscientious, and do our best to do right in the
world, and still the factual dimension can deal us an awful hand.
A wonderful house can be destroyed in a moment by an earth-
quake. A balanced and stable relationship can be stressed and
imbalanced with the onset of a sudden heart attack or disease.
Rights and privileges we take for granted may be taken away with

a change in government. Hard work to loosen the bonds of poverty does not guarantee escape from the ghetto. Facts do indeed impact the way we relate to one another, but many of them are beyond our control.

When a severe violation takes place in a family that damages trust and causes pain, there is a tendency to blame the circumstance on the facts that surround life. For instance, this report from a older woman who was severely abused by her mother deflected the responsibility for her mother's abuse by holding a circumstance responsible.

> It was tough for my mother. My father was gone and she chopped cotton to get a little money for us. She would come home so tired and worn out that any little thing would set her off. She would take it out on me, but she wouldn't have if we would have had a little more money. It would have been easier. It really wasn't her fault.

The question in this instance is, Whose fault was it? The woman was angry and upset about the abuse and it spilled onto her own children. No doubt that the financial stresses and lack of support from her father impacted her mother severely, but the circumstances themselves cannot deflect the responsibility for the abuse. The assumption that a change in circumstances would have changed the abuse does not alleviate the anger of the woman, it simply shifts the bulk of the anger to a dimension where humans do not have control and are not responsible. No matter what their factual status, humans are the only ones who can be held responsible for damage in relationships. Facts do impact the way we relate, but they do not excuse our responsibility to execute and fulfill our fair obligations in relationships.

Insight into the factual dimension allows a person to see facts with a clearer perspective. Although we may look at the facts of life and use them to understand how they have shaped a person who has done us damage, to blame our pain on the circumstances of life displaces our anger and pain onto a source that cannot be held responsible. If we are hurt by our family, our family is responsible to address the hurt. We kid ourselves if we believe that a change of circumstances or reality will alleviate the pain. Insight into facts that surround a violation in family trust should help in recognition of forces that shape behavior, but should also point out the reality that the circumstances are largely beyond human control and are not responsible for the violation itself. When we gain this insight, we stop looking to improvement in the factual dimension to ease our emotional pain or make relationships easier. In the same manner, we have the insight to not use our factual past or present circumstances to excuse our behavior in relationships.

## INSIGHT AND THE WORK OF FORGIVENESS

Some question whether insight is the work of forgiveness at all. There are indeed limits to insight in the work of forgiveness. Insight can give us an honest perspective of the family violation, help us recognize destructive situations so we can protect ourselves, help us believe that we are worthy and valued individuals despite harmful action taken toward us, and help us not blame our plight on circumstance, but it heals neither our sense of injustice nor the pain we feel from the drain of trust and love. Where is forgiveness in insight?

First, insight allows us to pinpoint the real cause of the violations we feel and protect ourselves from future damage. If trust in relationships is ever to be restored, victims of destructive violation must feel reasonably secure that they have some protection from being hurt the same way. Insight provides an initial step in this security. Second, insight provides us with a perspective to stop the destructive entitlement we feel from seeping into other relationships where we are potential victimizers of innocent people. When we experience pain, we rightly feel violated and feel that we deserve better. However, if we seek our entitlement from the wrong future relationships in manipulative and demanding ways, we damage others the same way we have been damaged ourselves. Insight provides the perspective to stop this revolving slate of destructive behavior.

Finally, insight is sometimes the only work of forgiveness that we can do. I am constantly amazed at how people who have been innocently violated in heinous ways are able to go on with life. Some of these people are cut off from the ones who performed the violation; others cannot put themselves back into the relationship with the victimizer because the victimizer would be destructive again. Suicides, murders, and torture are just a few of the painful violations that have left these individuals with drained resources of trust and doubts about love. But many of these people courageously go on and muddle through life. Insight for these people is not only the first station of forgiveness, it may be the only work of forgiveness that is possible for them to deal with the reality of the pain of the past, recognize how the violations were perpetuated, and stop the violation from occurring again.

*Chapter Three*

# STATION TWO: UNDERSTANDING

Although I certainly do not qualify as furniture refinisher, I have done some pieces of which I am quite proud. One of these is an old icebox, vintage late nineteenth century. I found it outside in a backyard; it was painted white with a black top. When I peeled off the first layer of white paint, beautiful oak wood was exposed and I could not help but thinking, "Why would anyone ever cover this fine wood with paint?" This antique icebox that had been discarded as unsalvageable now is coveted by many friends and family who visit my mother's house. There was a treasure underneath all of that messy paint, but it took some persistence to expose the beauty. But the question remained, What caused a person to damage such a fine piece?

The truth was that the icebox was discarded by someone in favor of a new refrigerator sometime in the 1940's. My mother bought the icebox because she and my father lived in a place without electricity. In keeping with the style of the time, my mother painted the icebox with white and black paint to make it have the appearance of a refrigerator—a real status symbol where they lived at the time. She and my father actually felt that they were doing something good to improve the condition of that awful old icebox. As the years went by, styles changed, but my parents simply never got around to restoring the icebox to its valued condition. The actions I considered unreasonable and irrational were actually well grounded in the best of intentions 50 years ago.

Much of the damage that takes place in families is similar. There were reasons and circumstances—no matter how unreasonable they now appear—for the actions and behavior that families took that caused individuals pain and hurt. The relationships may indeed look terrible and unsalvageable. However, almost all family relationships have real relational resources and strength. Understanding the situation and circumstances that influenced a family injustice and surrounded the person we hold responsible for our victimization can help us access this deeply rooted relational strength.

## GUILT AND EXONERATION

Insight allows us to stop future action and pain in the relationship with one who has injured us in some way and to end perpetual cycles of pain that we may inflict on innocent people because we are hurt. In short, insight gives us the ability to specify *how* damage occurred in a relationship so we can avoid damage in the future. *Understanding* differs from insight in that it gives us the ability to understand *why* the injustices, damage, and pain occurred. In answering the questions of why, understanding provides a mechanism that allows us to actually alleviate some of the pain and emotional turmoil that are caused by undeserved traumas.

When we have been inflicted with great harm by our family, the question of why cannot be forced from our minds. There is a standard within us that forces a reconciling of why a trusted family member would hurt an innocent party. How could a person who supposedly loved us treat us in such a way? What would cause anyone to do so much damage? Why did this happen to me? These questions of accountability prompt us to find justification for the actions against us. We hold the family member culpable because we trusted that person to treat us fairly and he or she did not. The injustice may be the result of tragic obligations that the family feels justified in demanding. For instance, an innocent young girl is sold into prostitution by her father to his coworkers. The injustice may also result from the family's ignoring its obligation to provide entitlement, which is the case with a child who was simply left deserted on the street. We hold the family member culpable and guilty for the injustice because we indeed believe that the family member is guilty of violating a standard of right. As one of my professors, John Drakeford, used to say, "You do not feel guilty, you *are* guilty." In turn, we hold the family member culpable because we internalized the action into a self-injury. To be victimized often means that we feel the action has made us dirty, unworthy, worthless, and undeserving. As a result, those of us who have been victimized consider the victimizing family members not only guilty for their actions but responsible *for the way they made us feel*. When we have been unjustly hurt, we hold the wrongdoers responsible for their guilt and our shame.

It is this guilt and shame that can cause such unrelenting emotional pain when we have been unjustly harmed. When we interpret that a person has been guilty of causing us an unjustified injury, we hold him or her responsible for total disregard for us. Depending on the injury, we may experience deep anger or even uncontrollable rage as the reality of undeserved hurt drives its message to us. We are driven by these forces to a disdain or even hate for the one who has wronged us.

Many times, this raging anger and hate separate us from the "real" person who has caused the injury, and instead make the person into an evil monster who is intentionally out to cause us grief. For instance, when we consider the heinous acts of men such as Hitler or Stalin, who were responsible for the murder of millions, we are much more likely to classify them as unthinking and unfeeling monsters who were out to destroy humanity. When we face the unbelievable magnitude of their guilt, we are insulted and enraged by their actions. We consider them evil, deviant, and disordered. They are no longer people, they are monsters. Such was the case with a young woman in recounting how the father deserted the family.

> He [the father] is a sleaze ball! He took everything that was good in our family and threw it all away so he could run away with his whore. We would all be better off if he was dead. I wish he was dead! He is evil and we need to just write him off!

The problem with classifying people as monsters is that we may consider monsters outside the reach of reason, and therefore it may be difficult to hold them responsible for their actions as people. In short, we cannot understand why a monster harmed us in an unjustified way because an evil, unthinking, unfeeling monster has no reason for doing harm. The only thing left to do is to kill the monster. However, even killing the monster does nothing to alleviate the unjustified pain and suffering the monster caused. We become trapped into a cycle of rage with no possibility of answering the question of why such an unjustified action occurred.

People are not monsters. Each person has a circumstance and reality that shape behavior. Humanity is indeed capable of horrendous evil and unjustified acts, but no human is beyond reason or, more importantly, responsibility. When we force the question of why unjustified actions were taken against us, we continue to hold a *person* responsible for guilt. The desire that we have to understand why someone would harm an innocent party in an undeserved way is the effort to hold a person accountable for his or her actions. This is true with all of humanity, but is especially salient with members of our families who have dealt us undeserved hurts. A man who repeatedly and viciously beats his wife and then takes his adolescent daughter out and sexually abuses her is responsible for tremendous damage. The wife's and daughter's instincts initially may leave them little room to imagine any circumstance in which to understand his actions. They may believe the man to be vile and dangerous and may be filled with rage over his irresponsibility. But if they consider him to be unreasoned, then they put him outside the reach of humanity.

The husband-father is not a monster. Most likely, he is an ordinary person who has been affected by irregular and harsh circumstances of life and relationships. It is only when we understand these irregular and harsh circumstances that we have the opportunity to help him and assist the wife and daughter in dealing with the problem of how a person who was trusted to love could cause such harm. Therefore, understanding is a necessary component in order to hold the wrongdoer responsible for his or her guilt and deal with the emotional pain that is caused by undeserved emotional damage in a family.

When coupled with the first station of insight, understanding allows us to accomplish the work of exoneration. Exoneration means that we achieve the insight necessary to protect ourselves and innocent parties from further relational damage and understand the circumstances of the person who caused us the unjustified pain. This combination helps us lift the load of culpability off the person who caused us the unjustified pain.

When we exonerate a family member who harmed us, we are not proclaiming the person trustworthy for the future. Indeed, the family member may be just as destructive as ever. However, insight achieved in the process of exoneration makes the wrongdoer less powerful because the victim is able to prevent the destructive situations from occurring again. Also, when we exonerate a victimizing family member, we are not excusing the person from responsibility for the action. Undeserved and unjustified action remains undeserved and unjustified. When we seek to understand the injustices and pain, in essence we are identifying ourselves with a similar circumstance experienced by the wrongdoer.

In the process of exonerating we come to understand and appreciate the wrongdoer's situation, options, efforts, and limits and see our own fallibility in dealing with such circumstances. This understanding achieved in the process of exoneration leads the victim to a position where he or she need not condemn the victimizer as a monster in order to deal with the problems caused by guilt. The victim's identification with and understanding of the victimizing family member allows the victim without condemnation to resolve the question of how a trusted loved one could cause such unjustified pain. As this question is resolved, the internalized pain from the past injustice has potential to fade. Neither victim nor victimizer is "bad," but the situations and limits of both contributed to an unjustified wound to real and fragile people. Exoneration releases the victim and victimizer from condemnation, but does not make the relationship trustworthy and does not release the victimizer from responsibility of causing the hurt.

In order to achieve exoneration in the work of forgiveness, a victim must learn to master the injustice that caused pain with both *power* and *identification*. Insight provides power to stop the injustice. But preventing future relational injustices in the family is only part of exonerating. Complete exoneration involves relieving the wrongdoer of the heavy burden of condemnation for the damage and hurt that he or she has caused. Releasing the victimizer from condemnation requires care and attention that come from identification. Identification in turn eases emotional turmoil by resolving how and why unjustified actions occurred. Understanding provides identification to stop the pain caused by past injustices.

## UNDERSTANDING

Victimization takes a heavy toll on family relationships not only in terms of justice and trust, but also in terms of the relative position of members giving and receiving from one another. A family member who is guilty of using or abusing me in some way violated a justified balance of obligations and entitlements. In other words, since the family member abused me, I did not get what I fairly deserved from the relationship and the person is indebted to me. In essence, the person owes me compensation for the harm done, not to mention the just entitlement I may not receive from the relationship. This puts me in a one-up position to the person who victimized me and is indebted to me. This one-up, one-down position of family members in relation to one another can significantly deteriorate the relational security and emotional stability of persons in both positions.

From the one-up position of victimized unjustly, one might feel that one is in the position of judge of the victimizer. If the victimizer is judged guilty, then right is on the side of the victimized. Scrutinization of the action and condemnation of the wrongdoer may be a result of the superior position of the victim. On the other hand, from the one-down position of the victimizer, one might feel attacked for the damaging actions. There are almost always mitigating circumstances that shed light even on the most unjustified actions against innocent parties. If the victimizer feels that he or she does not get a fair hearing for the circumstances and experiences that surrounded the damage—or, more importantly, have an opportunity to express the injustice that has been experienced by him or her—then an unrelenting defensive posture may be the result. Every accusation by the victimized person is answered or thwarted by an attack, excuse, or misdirection by the person who caused the pain. Exoneration from this one-up, one-down positioning is extremely difficult.

Understanding, the second station of forgiveness, completes the work of exonerating the one from culpability for unjustly hurting us. If I understand the wrongdoer in terms of his or her position, limitations, development, efforts, and intent, I achieve an identification with the person. This identification is essential in that it acknowledges the fallibility of every human being. When I understand the family member who has unjustly used or manipulated me, *I acknowledge that if I were placed in the same situation, with the wrongdoer's position, limitations, and development, I might not do any better.* In essence, if I were in the victimizer's shoes, I might make some of the same mistakes and cause the same hurt.

This is the crux of understanding in the work of forgiveness. It stabilizes the relative position of victim and victimizer in relation to one another. An understanding victim, even when he or she has experienced extreme injustice, feels a reduction of blame and is no longer one-up. An understood victimizer, no matter how awful the act of abuse, is likely to feel less defensive and is no longer one-down. Responsibility is not lifted from the wrongdoer, but understanding achieves exoneration and removes the condemnation and blame.

## Understanding and the Dimension of Relational Ethics

One of my real joys in astronomy is to search the sky for what are known as "deep sky" objects. These are very faint galaxies, nebulae, or star clusters that are thousands of light years from the earth. When I catch a small smudge of light through my telescope, I am exhilarated to realize that the light that I currently am seeing is actually light from thousands of years ago. Because of the distance between the earth and the heavens, I am in the here-and-now currently experiencing an event that took place millennia ago. It is a very elemental experience in Einstein's realm of relativity. Time and space are funny things.

Time and space also do funny things in family relationships. As I sit and watch a family with a particularly destructive bent or hear stories of seemingly intentional and dramatic damage, most of the time I am experiencing family relativity. The physical abuse, incest, neglect, trauma, or addiction that I see in the here-and-now often is a message from the past injustices that have been experienced by the one who has perpetrated the violence or abuse. If I look at the damage only from a here-and-now perspective, it will be difficult for me to see anything but a victim and a victimizer. It is only when I step back and remember that the past experiences in our family relationships often play themselves out in the here-and-now that I have an opportunity to understand the original source of the distress and injustice that led a victim to become a victimizer.

To achieve understanding in the dimension of relational ethics, the one who has suffered the pain or injury from another family member must reckon with the pain and injury that may have been experienced by the wrongdoer. As we have discussed earlier, most family damage and injustice are passed along from generation to generation in what Boszormenyi-Nagy and Spark (1984) refer to as a *revolving slate*. If I do not get the love, nurturing and security that I am justly entitled to in my family and am used, abused, and manipulated in fulfilling obligations that are not appropriate or fair, I will possibly go on a self-justifying bend to get what I deserve. In most cases, these self-justifying and destructive actions are taken on innocent parties such as spouses and children.

The dynamic truth about the revolving slate is that the person who is the victimizer actually feels justified in the destructive action. Family members who damage others do not usually do so randomly—they do it because they feel violated, cheated, and damaged. Victimizers feel justified in or *deserving* of the behavior, even though they may at the same time despise its effects on others. The effect of this revolving slate on the abuser's sense of justification is seen in the story of a middle-aged mother who was sexually abused as a young girl.

> The only person I feel I can trust is my 6-year-old daughter. She takes care of me—combs my hair and cooks for me. Most nights I end up sleeping with her just so she can tell me everything is alright. Sometimes I cry for hours. My daughter won't hardly leave me anymore because she doesn't want me to be alone. I know that I shouldn't expect so much of her and I should let her be a kid, but I really do need her to take care of me. All of the awful things I've been through, I feel like I have at least earned the love of my daughter.

As a result of the mother's experience of sexual abuse, she clearly parentifies her daughter, expecting the daughter to provide her with love and security in an adult fashion. As much as the mother dislikes using the daughter in this manner, she states that her past has earned her the entitlement to her daughter's love and nurturing. In short, the mother feels justified. However, the daughter will never experience the love and nurturing of a mother and will in fact be obligated to fulfill an adult role with her mother in highly inappropriate ways. The daughter will be subject to the same revolving slate of injustice as she will feel one day deserving of the love and nurturing that she missed out from her mother. Who will give her this love and nurturing? Most likely she will seek to get it from her children who are yet unborn. My colleague Glen Jennings sums up this concept of the revolving slate with the statement, "It's like having a script with the wrong actors." In other words, the great play *Romeo and Juliet* can never be played out successfully with the actors of *Othello*. The play will not be done justice, and the actors will be nothing but frustrated.

Once the person who has experienced the undeserved hurt understands the injustices and revolving slate in the wrongdoer's past, identification with the turmoil and pain of the wrongdoer is easier. This identification with the wrongdoer does not suddenly make the injustice right or make the wrongdoer trustworthy. But understanding in this relational ethics dimension does make for significant strides in answering the question of why one who was trusted to love damaged the relationship. As this question of why is answered, it is not unusual for the rage and pain that a victim may feel to subside, as was the case with a woman who was severely physically abused by her mother.

> My mother came from a crazy family. Her father forced
> the children to steal food. He disciplined the children by
> tying them to fence posts, beating them, and then leaving
> them for the rest of the day. When I didn't do what my
> mother wanted, she sort of kicked into a rage. She was
> dangerous and crazy, but I think I even knew then that it
> was not really her. She probably felt so much pain that she
> didn't know what else to do. But even with what she did
> to me, I think she experienced worse. Maybe I'm just in

denial, but I think my mother did do the best she could considering what happened to her.

## Understanding and the Dimension of Family Transactions

As painful as it was to come from an abusive family, I experience more pain in my life from my own abusive tendencies. As I mentioned before, one of my self-justifying solutions to my painful abusive past was to emphatically declare that I would never have children:  thus denying my parents future offspring and ensuring that I would have all of my wife's affections for myself. But my own revolving slate of past injustices seeped out in even more overt and disturbing ways.  For instance, I am person who takes great joy in a joke or a tease.  It is fun for me to play practical jokes, banter, and roughhouse with loved ones in my family.  But before I worked on so many of the issues between me and my parents, I would often find my play and teasing getting distinctly out of hand.  My words would often turn to vicious sarcasm.  My playful tickle would sometimes turn into forceful domination.  On several occasions with my wife, I would tickle or "goose" her in such a way that it would hurt, to the point that she would angrily respond with tears in her eyes demanding that I stop.

I would stop.  But to be honest, my feeling at the time was that I wanted to do it again.  It was a strange compelling thought.  Here was the woman I loved telling me to stop something that hurt her and I wanted to hurt her again.  It was as if I was telling myself, "I will do what I want to.  I have a right.  Teasing and hurting are what I want to do."  I wanted to stop and I wanted to continue.  I would have never considered myself abusive to my wife because I never hit her or threw something at her, but here I was using my power to hurt her.  The truth was, I was being abusive to her.  The abuse was just coming out in a transaction that I did not recognize at the time.

The objectifiable nature of the dimension of family transactions often leads us to think that actions of family members stand alone and are disconnected to the family system.  But by and large, the transactions in the family are a result of the influences that we experience. Even in the best of family situations, members often find themselves saying or doing things to one another the destructive potential of which surprises or even shocks them. When we have experienced extreme family pain, the pain finds its way eventually into transactions. Understanding of and identification with the original family pain can make sense of seemingly unrelated actions by a family member who unjustly hurts another. This was the case of a young woman who suffered years of verbal abuse from her mother concerning her sexuality.

> I remember going out to play and my mother accusing me of masturbating on the playground equipment. She would focus on every thing I wore and would accuse me of trying to be seductive and then would call me a tramp or a whore. As I got older, I realized that she would attack me every time I was noticed by another male. It wasn't until years later that I found out that she had been sexually abused and she blamed herself. She would accuse me of being loose because she was afraid I would be abused.

The greatest effect of understanding in this dimension, however, is seen in the transactions of the person who has been unjustly victimized by another. A victim often sees the transactions that were used to hurt him or her as the source of pain. However, it is the *power* and *law* or rule systems that are perpetuated by transactions that actually assault our sense of family justice and trust. Because we feel the injustice, we are prone to use this same power and the same family rules to gain our entitlement from innocent parties. Our actions or the family transactions may be different, but the power and rules utilized in the transaction are the same. My abusive teasing was stimulated by the same transactional base as my parents' physical abuse. This is also seen in the story of an older man who was accused by his family of being a workaholic.

My father was a real boozer. I don't think he ever held one
job in his life. I swore that I would never be like him—that
I would make something of myself. So I worked all the
time. Now my daughter tells me that I never gave her
anything. I thought I was a great father because I
provided. Now I find out that my daughter got the same
thing from me as I got from my father—nothing. She has
a point.

The value of such understanding in the dimension of family
transactions is that when we see our own actions connected to the
actions of one who has harmed us, we achieve a greater sense of
identification. Additionally and more importantly, we are also
able to view our transactions with our current family members in
a clearer and overt manner where our own destructive behavior is
less likely to seep out.

## Understanding and the Dimension of Individual Psychology

One of the things that I am constantly amazed at in my
therapeutic practice is how persons who have unreasonably and
unjustly suffered at the hands of a family member will many times
blame themselves for the abuse or feel that they deserve such
retribution. Those who suffer unjust pain from a family member
often will take the destructive entitlement out on someone else, as
we have discussed. However, many times victims will take the
destructive entitlement out on another innocent party—their own
psyche.

The loyalty that we feel toward our family is very powerful by
the fact that our family is the place where we come into being and
find out all that we know about ourselves. Violent and abusive acts
fly in the face of this supposedly trustworthy and safe environment. In dealing with the responsibility for such an inconsistency
as a destructive and damaging act in the family, victims often
internalize brutality or abuse as something that they deserve or

even that they caused. This was the case for a teenage girl who had been brutalized by her father.

> It was my fault. I could tell when he was having a bad time and he was about to explode. Sometimes I would just get so tired of him yelling and screaming that I would say or do something to set him off. He would beat me, but I was the one who actually started it.

In essence, instead of making the father responsible for the guilt of unjustified actions that caused pain, the daughter took on the guilt and held herself responsible. There is a heavy toll for taking on this responsibility. As victims accuse themselves of deserving such abuse, they are infiltrated with shame, unworthy of normal interactions. Instead of turning the result of injustice into a feeling of rage and assuming the father is a monster, the daughter turns the responsibility for the injustice inward and she feels shame and worthlessness. Victims who suffer self-degradation from taking on the guilt of irresponsible family acts often then look for opportunities that confirm their self-perception. Instead of striving for love and recognition, these individuals' lives become chaotic as they feel that pain and accusations are part of life's acceptable response to their being.

Understanding in this dimension is particularly necessary in order to salvage the victim's individual psyche. As victims begin to understand the motives, situations, efforts, and *responsibility* of the individuals who victimized them, the more they understand that the destructive action has more to do with the victimizers than it does with them. Instead of internalizing the pain and guilt to beliefs about themselves, they are better able to externalize the damage. Instead of believing themselves unworthy, they are better able to see themselves as victims. Breaking through this barrier of shame and pain is often difficult because individuals may construct complex psychological defenses to deal with such brutality. For instance, the following is an account from a woman who possibly had multiple personalities in response to repeated sexual abuse.

> I'm scared. (*long pause*) When I start believing that I'm okay I start remembering things that scare me. I remember being raped. (*long pause*) I think I remember setting fire to the guy's car who raped me. Sometimes I think it may be easier to just be depressed and not remember.

Understanding is the powerful tool that allows an individual to start objectifying the introjected image that the unjustified act caused in his or her psyche. Although this is often difficult, the result is not only a greater understanding of one's own self but also a greater potential for understanding the real motives and situations surrounding the person who really was responsible for the unjust action.

### Understanding in the Dimension of Facts

Understanding in the dimension of facts is usually brought about through identification with the circumstances of the wrongdoer. When I understand the factors of health, culture, and situation on a person who abused me, I am able to sympathize with the stress or circumstance that may have contributed to that person's perpetrating the damage on me. Identification with these facts acknowledges the victimizer's struggle and therefore credits his or her situation. Many times, people do the best they can in intolerable circumstances. Such was the case of a middle-aged man explaining the facts surrounding his depression and subsequent neglect of and withdrawal from the family to his son.

> I came back from the war and I thought I was going crazy. Half of the time I wanted to kill myself, and half the time I thought I was going to kill all of you [the family]. I didn't

> know what to do. I didn't know that you were supposed
> to talk about these things. So I withdrew. I thought I
> wouldn't hurt all of you if I just stayed away.

Certainly the pain and stresses of this man's situation dictated his actions toward his family. Considering the consequences of a possible suicide/murder or of withdrawal and depression, he opted for what he saw as the lesser of two evils. In this particular case, when the son heard the facts surrounding the disturbing life of his father, he was better able to understand the father's actions. He responded to his father by stating that he believed the father did the best he could under the circumstances and given the limitations of his knowledge. This identification between the son and the father then credited the father and enabled both to resolve some of the unspoken pain and grief that they had carried in the family for years.

Although the factual dimension can set the stage for and contribute greatly to the damage that family members perpetrate on one another, it is not responsible for the damage in and of itself. The world is created neutral to good or harm. For instance, the piece of lumber that I can use to constructively build a house I can also use to beat a person to death. The piece of lumber is neither good nor evil, it is dependent upon my utilization. In the end, family members are still responsible for their actions in their families. But understanding the facts surrounding abusive or brutal actions contributes to a more balanced picture of the efforts and intentions of one who victimized another.

## UNDERSTANDING AND
## THE WORK OF FORGIVENESS

Understanding in the work of forgiveness is much like that of the stage and sound people at a concert. Most of their work goes on long before the concert begins and continues long after it is over. If their job is done correctly, the people in the audience rarely notice them. Understanding is mostly internalized work. It does not require that the person victimized join into a relationship with the family member who caused pain or even that the victim directly communicate with the victimizer. But as understanding of the victimizer and circumstances surrounding the unjustified action becomes clearer to the victim, so does the potential for dealing with internal pain caused by the victimization. This in turn sets in motion several aspects of forgiveness.

First, understanding allows us to confront the possible rage and anger we feel toward the victimizer by helping us identify with the injustices that the victimizer experienced in the past. This helps us answer the question of why, and see the wrongdoer as a fragile and damaged person instead of a raging monster. We are able to lift the load of hate from the wrongdoer because we acknowledge that the victimizer was also once a victim. In this manner, we accomplish the work of exonerating the victimizer of evil intent and free ourselves from rage.

Second, understanding gives us the ability to acknowledge the difficult issues of responsibility. Family members who have hurt us usually did not do so because they were intentionally bent on hurting us. Most often, our victimizers are people who made tragic and awful mistakes while trying to do the best they could. As we understand them as people, we can rightly consider in a rational and balanced manner their part in the damage that they perpetrated on us.

Finally and most importantly, understanding achieves the work of forgiveness in that as we make identification with the one who has hurt us and exonerate that person from our condemnation, we are able to relieve much of our burden of shame and pain. Through exoneration, we not only release the victimizer from the load of culpability, we release ourselves from the load of feeling unlovely and unworthy.

*Chapter Four*

# STATION THREE: GIVING THE OPPORTUNITY FOR COMPENSATION

W hen *Apollo 8* took off for its lunar orbital flight in 1968, the United States had become an old hand at orbital flights around the earth. But this mission was something special. This mission was the first time that humans would venture away from earth on a new rocket that would take them some 238,000 miles away. New techniques and equipment meant new risks and potential tragedies. After lift-off, there was a point where the crew fired a rocket that propelled them toward the moon. After the rocket was fired, they were on their way—all the way to the moon. The problem was that after the point when the commitment was made to go for the moon, there was no turning back. The crew would have to travel all the way to the moon before they could turn around and traverse back to earth.

Family life presents all of us with very similar choices through-out our life courses. Marriages, friendships, parenthood, job decisions, financial obligations, are just a few of the options that present themselves. In most cases, the options bring us new risks and potential tragedies. But once the decisions are made, the new commitments and obligations become intertwined with the existing parts of our lives and we are changed and modified in ways we could not have imagined. In most cases, we cannot go back on the decisions before the impact of the risks affects us.

In the work of forgiveness, there is also a line of decision that exists between exonerating and forgiving. Forgiving people who have injured us unjustly sets us on a course that engages us into a relationship with the very people who caused us so much pain. The decision to begin the process of forgiving brings an unpredictable amount of risks as we expose ourselves to potential new damage. But as in most of life's decisions, there is tremendous potential payoff if forgiving can be accomplished. This work of forgiving is accomplished two ways: through *giving the opportunity for compensation* and through *the overt act of forgiving*.

## THE VALUE OF FORGIVING

For some people who have suffered hurts that they did not deserve, exoneration achieved through insight and understanding is the limit of the work of forgiveness. Insight helps empower persons who carry family hurt and injustice to see the root of their pain and relieves their burden of transferring the injustice to other relationships. In situations where victims are cut off from the information about the person who did them harm or where the wrongdoer is still dangerous or vicious, insight is the limit of what can be done in order to move on with life. Understanding, the next station, enables the innocent victims to identify with the situations and circumstances that surrounded their victimizers and can calm their emotional turmoil that echoes from the past. Where it is possible, understanding is better, because it puts the one who experienced the harm in touch with the reality of the real person who was the victimizer. Whether or not the victim and the victimizer actually have physical contact, there is an emotional confrontation of the issues surrounding the injustice against family obligation.

In understanding, victims are closer to the story and circumstance of the family member who treated them unjustly, but need not be in physical contact. Understanding is internalized work done on the part of the person who is wronged. If the family member who caused the injury is still dangerous, unreliable, manipulative, or unreasonable, the victim is able to keep sufficient protective distance. So in exonerating family members who have caused injury, individuals deal with the past in such a way that the burden of injustice need not be carried to the future, but they are not put back into relationship with one who has done them harm. In many cases, limiting the work of forgiveness to exonerating is not only wise, but the only thing that can be done.

Some have argued that the releasing of culpability that is accomplished in exoneration is forgiveness. The dictionary defines the word *forgive* as "to cease to feel resentment against an offender." In the literature on forgiveness in the therapeutic and religious community, the idea of releasing resentment's being forgiveness is common, although it is somewhat sketchy on details of releasing such condemnation. But what is just as common in this literature is the implication that forgiveness also requires reconciliation and rejoining of relationship. For example, Schneider (1989) reviews a process of forgiving a sexually compulsive person that includes recognizing the wrong done by the compulsive person, recognizing the imperfections on both sides, and joining into a relationship with the person that does not tolerate unacceptable behavior. T. E. Smith (1991) discusses the ideas of forgiving and the concepts of reconciliation of relationships. This idea of reconciliation and reconnection is also discussed by Levy, Joyce, and List (1988) as it applies to parents and adolescents who were residents in an acute care psychiatric hospital. On a more philosophical level, Todd (1985) discusses Jung's ideas on confession, forgiveness, and reconciliation, while Vande Kemp (1987) draws parallels of contextual ideas of forgiveness and rejunction in the works of Charles Williams. Many religious writers (e.g., Smedes, 1984; Augsburger, 1981; Patton, 1985; Pingleton, 1989) discuss forgiveness as a process or as stages by which one confronts the past, deals with the hurt or injustice by canceling out guilt and debt, and reconciles or comes together with the other in a manner that is representative of the healing. Although release of resentment is essential in the work of forgiveness, many clearly believe that it also involves some reestablishment of relationship. But why would any person who was violated and damaged by a member of his or her family ever want to enter back into a relationship that caused the hurt?

The reason that reestablishment of the family relationship is preferable, where it is possible, is that these relationships are the only way available to us to solve the problem of responsibility and erase the pain of the violation. As previously discussed, the root of family pain is the severe violation of fairness or justice that leads us to believe that we are unloved and that our family is not trustworthy. In Buber's (1970) framework, we exist in a context of an *I-Thou* relationship. In other words, without the experience of relating to, giving to, and receiving from another person, we have an insufficient basis to experience emotions and thought. In order to experience self-understanding and self-delineation as *I*, I must be in the context of relating to *Thou*. This mandatory relational context stimulates beings to be responsible in their enacting of balance and exchange through giving and receiving in reciprocal ways.

But it is not only that I exist in an *I-Thou* context, I also come from parents in an *I-Thou* context and will propagate my family from an *I-Thou* context. As Boszormenyi-Nagy (1986) has discussed, individuals always exist within the framework of three generations. The implications of Buber's philosophy are that I simultaneously carry responsibility for fair and justified relating in three directions: (1) with the generation from which I came; (2) with the generation of my equals such as siblings, friends, and spouses; and (3) with the generation of posterity. Because we were created out of family relationships, we are ethicallly bound to responsibly perpetuate our family relationships. Whether in the context of family or not, in Erikson's (1985) terms, we have a responsibility for generativity for the sake of posterity.

When a family member violates or injures me in some unjustified way, my self-perception and image become skewed. I have been violated in the *I-Thou* context from which I came, and the love and trust to which I am entitled have evaporated. However, even if I am damaged unfairly, I still carry the responsibility for fair relating within the context of relationship with others; such is the nature of the *I-Thou* context. In order to carry forth my responsibility toward my relationships of equal status and posterity unhindered, I must be treated in a ethical manner by my family.

By using insight and understanding to exonerate my family that was not trustworthy and did not love me, I can certainly ease my pain and shame and achieve remarkable responsibility in the way I relate to others, but I will still have the nagging reality of the injustice received. I can stop myself from reeling under the pain of hurts I have received or from committing injustices to others, but I will do so out of a self-gauging activity of checking myself. While certainly possible and more desirable than destructive behavior, relaxed freedom in giving, receiving, and trusting others may be difficult. In short, I must know that my family loves me and that they are trustworthy in order to have the responsibility and pain in my life sufficiently addressed where they do not hinder my relationship with others.

One of the wonderful things about this three-generation context in which we exist is that there are many opportunities for family members to address the past abuses that they received. I am a grown man, but I still carry with me the feelings and many of the perceptions of that 8-year-old boy who came to the conclusion that his family did not love him and would be better off without him. My parents and I cannot go back to the past and do things differently, but who my parents were and who I was are still a part of *us*. That 8-year-old who experienced an awful and abusive violation is still in me and is still available. Although neither I nor my parents can go back in time, we can address the past violations in the here-and-now.   When that part of me that is eight experiences a redress of those love and trust issues with my parents in the here and now and I get the love and trust I deserve, I become whole and freer to execute my responsibility to them, my wife, and my children.

This is what the process of forgiving is about.  It means that we return to the relational issues as they were when they caused us so much damage.  When we arrive on the emotional scene where the love and trust were violated in our families, we open ourselves up to the possibility that whoever hurt us unjustly is now—at least in part—able to give us what we deserve.  We build a bridge across the violation in order that our victimizer may address the damage in a trustworthy and loving manner.  In this way, the process of forgiving is really a rebirth of the relationship.  Forgiving provides a way for the entitlement of love and trust in a family to be restored, even if the love and trust have never been exhibited.  Exonerating provides insight that gives us the power to stop future injustice, and understanding that gives identification that eases our pain, but it does not restore the relationship and reestablish the possibility of love and trust in the family.  Forgiving is a unique human possibility that has the potential of not only *easing* our pain from the past but also *healing* it.

There are two paths that one may choose in this methodology of forgiving—both are equal in their process orientation and effectiveness in restoring broken relationships.  *In giving the opportunity for compensation*, the victim provides the opportunity for the victimizer to "prove" that he or she is loving and trustworthy by allowing interactions that make both vulnerable. The original unjust and destructive actions may or may not ever be directly discussed between the injured and injuring party.  *The overt act of forgiveness* differs in that the violation is directly addressed between the two parties and responsibility and promise of restored relationship are clearly delineated.  Both paths require time and trustworthy relating in the future between the two parties in order for the damaged part of the relationship to heal.  The two paths may build on one another; a person who gives a wrongdoer the opportunity for compensation may eventually engage in the overt act of forgiveness. However, the two paths may also be exclusive.

It is true that the process of forgiving has almost miraculous potential to heal relationships, but the potential is bought at a very high cost. The work of forgiving demands that we enter back into the relationship with the very people who hurt us unjustly. This risk is not to be taken lightly and is difficult to negotiate. How do I put myself at risk with a family member who I may feel does not love me and whom I cannot trust? If I take the risk, it will mean that I am vulnerable and the person may choose to abuse, use, or manipulate me again. Among the many misconceptions about the work of forgiveness that you hear is that those who do not forgive only do damage to themselves. I suppose there is a thread of truth to this idea in that if I am enraged or bitter over the injustice, it can ruin my psyche and my other relationships. But if I cross the line of exonerating into the process of forgiving, I have something very real to lose. I may be violated again, which holds the potential for making my pain worse. This means that I must consider carefully whether I want to move from exonerating into forgiving.

Unfortunately, there is no way of knowing for sure whether the future relationship may be healing or continue to be destructive. The best I can do is to evaluate the potential process of forgiving and healing in the relationship based on three criteria. First, I must judge whether I am willing to have the injustice addressed and have my pain healed. If my life is chaotic and unstable and I am filled with anger and rage against the one who has hurt me, I may be unwilling to accept my victimizer's offer of love and trust. Second, I must judge whether the continuation or healing of the relationship is necessary or important to me. I may be hurt from the relationship when I become vulnerable. It is only if the relationship is judged essential to me that I will be able to put myself at the risk necessary to reestablish love and trust. Finally, I must make some evaluation of the readiness of the person who unjustly and destructively damaged me to now love me and treat me in a trustworthy manner. This is more difficult to know and evaluate because we do not truly know the thoughts and emotions of another and we may be fearful of our victimizers. However, there are tip-offs to how forgiving may proceed. On the one hand, there may be a softening of attitudes or efforts toward reconnection may be well received. On the other hand, abuse or manipulation may be as severe as ever. There is no glory or healing in putting oneself at risk for the process of forgiving if the victimizer promises to be as unjust and damaging as before. Exonerating in the work of forgiveness is much more beneficial if forgiving and reestablishing a relationship are a lost cause. There are some family relationships where the threat of continuing unjust and destructive behavior is so severe that the process of forgiving would be a lost cause.

## PREREQUISITES FOR FORGIVING

The work of forgiveness happens in many ways and at different rates of speed and intensity for different people. The work of forgiveness indeed proceeds a little at a time over a long period of time. It is important to reemphasize here that the work of forgiveness does not proceed along four *stages*. As outlined in this book, forgiveness is achieved along four *stations*. It is most likely that as the work of exonerating and forgiving proceeds, we oscillate between the stations of insight, understanding, giving the opportunity for compensation, and the overt act of forgiveness many times and gradually are able to exonerate and forgive more and more. So when we discuss prerequisites for forgiving, we are not stating these as absolute requirements before the process of forgiving can be initiated. These prerequisites are offered simply as indicators or predictors of success in the forgiving process. Their presence should enhance the effort of forgiving, but their absence does not mean that forgiving is not possible.

### Exoneration

Even though exoneration is not a requirement, there is little doubt that exonerating the person who has unjustly caused damage does much to enhance the process of forgiving. First, insight achieved in exoneration gives the victim the ability to detail just what violation occurred. Instead of the violation's remaining nebulous, and difficult for both the wronged and the wrongdoer to address, the specifics concerning the hurt and damage are delineated. Second, insight provides the victim with the power to protect against damaging transactions. Without this ability to protect oneself, the victim will proceed back into the relationship with the victimizer with tentativeness and fear, which may overwhelm the effort to achieve the vulnerability necessary for forgiving. Finally, understanding achieved in exoneration alleviates much of the emotional distress of the one who has unjustly suffered wrongs from another. Forgiving is very difficult if hindered with unbridled rage or anger over past hurts or self-defeating blame or depression.

## Acceptance

When any severe damage or tragedy occurs, there is a tendency on all our parts to play a game of what ifs. We second-guess motives, situations, and actions and wonder about different realities if things had been different. It is part of the process we go through when we hurt and mourn. However, when we have suffered unjust tragedy or damage in the context of family, we need to accept the fact that the damage occurred and that it has left scars. If we get stuck in the framework of mourning the damage, we become immobilized in our efforts to heal. Acceptance means that we see ourselves as innocent victims of others' unjust behavior and that we hold them accountable for their actions. This is not the same as blaming; it is simply recognizing and accepting the fact that there has been a true violation that must be addressed by both parties.

## Willingness

Willingness to involve oneself in the process of forgiving means that a person has come to the point where he or she is reasonably sure about being able to release the wrongdoer from the responsibility for the irresponsible or intentional damage. Too often, people will pursue a relationship with their victimizer only to accuse the wrongdoer of the damage done. In many of these cases, even when the wrongdoer asks for forgiveness accepting full responsibility for his or her actions and promising to be trustworthy, the victim finds himself or herself in a position of being unwilling to forgive. Willingness to forgive requires that the victim be reasonably sure of being able to pursue a continuing relationship with the victimizer without the need to hold the violation over the victimizer's head forever.

## Realism

People are imperfect. When we enter into the realm of forgiving a person who caused us damage and pain we need to be realistic in our expectations of ourselves and our victimizers. We will say we forgive the person who caused us pain, only to discover later that a memory or situation will trigger anger or depression again. People whom we have forgiven will make mistakes both intentional and unintentional that will bring us pain and make us question whether or not the effort of forgiving was true and sincere. Being realistic about the process of forgiving means that one will acknowledge that a damaged relationship will not be perfect. Many times the relationship will take "one step forward, two steps back" as both the wronged and the wrongdoer learn how to relate to one another in a loving and trustworthy manner.

## Commitment

As one can imagine, the process of forgiving a person who was responsible for heinous and horrendous crimes against our being is alarming and threatening. The risk is real, and the hazards in rebirthing a relationship between ourselves and our victimizer are many. Therefore, one must be convinced of the value of pursuing such a restoration of relationship and that it is indeed necessary. One who believes that a family relationship is optional or not desirable will eventually lack the commitment necessary to make the healing of the relationship possible. Only when we feel that the reestablishment of the relationship is necessary for our own well–being and for posterity will we have the commitment necessary to actually reconnect. There is little gray area in the decision to pursue forgiving. We either reconnect or we do not.

## GIVING THE OPPORTUNITY FOR COMPENSATION

Once when I was helping my father with some work on heavy machinery, I turned a mechanism that badly sliced his thumb. I was a teenager at the time, and amidst the blood and pain of my father, I did not exactly know what to do. When my father regained his composure, he carefully directed me step-by-step on how to administer first aid and then how to get him to a doctor. I had caused the injury, but I was also the one who treated the wound. This was difficult enough for me, but imagine how it was for my father as he had to make his wound vulnerable for treatment to the very person who had harmed him.

The third station along the road of forgiveness, giving the opportunity for compensation, presents this kind of perplexing dilemma to those who have been unjustly harmed by another. The work of forgiveness is accomplished in this station by the victim's allowing the victimizer to rebuild the status of love and trust in the relationship in a progressive manner that eventually erases the gravity of the injustice in the face of present balanced interactions. This process is distinctly different from the victim's demanding that the culprit apologize or ask forgiveness for the injury. Indeed, in many of the situations in which a victim has forgiven the person who caused the damage using this process, the wrongdoer had little or no knowledge of how the violation had hurt the victim. In the process of compensation, the relationship between the wronged and wrongdoer proceeds on a step-by-step, interaction-by-interaction basis.

A victim's giving the victimizer the opportunity for compensation is like a bank giving small credit lines to previously financially irresponsible individuals. The more the person who victimized an innocent party demonstrates ability to give and receive in a balanced and fair way, the more vulnerable and trusting the victim is willing to be in order to give the victimizer a chance. It simply means giving those who have perpetrated undeserved hurts in the past the chance to prove that they will not do it again and are capable of love and worthy of trust. Again, in this process trustworthiness is usually established a little at a time over a long period of time. As family members responsibly execute love and trustworthiness in this second chance, they develop more and more resources of love and trust. These resources in the here and now then address the undeserved hurts in the past, and the pain has potential for being healed. Individuals in families become empowered by demonstrated commitment and responsibility to justice in the family, which leads to even more committed and responsible behavior.

Many people choose to pursue the work of forgiveness in this third station because, in many ways, it maximizes the benefits of relational healing while minimizing the potential damage one may suffer from entering back into a relationship with a family member who has done damage. First, giving the opportunity for compensation does not demand that the damage be verbally addressed by victim and victimizer. This provides both with a nondefensive posture where a potentially destructive cycle of accusation and denial or counteraccusation won't transpire. Second, because this third station is based on the relational culprit's ability to be loving and trustworthy in the present, initial forays into the relationship by the one who has been damaged can be small, planned, and gauged. This allows the victim to present a small opportunity to the untrustworthy family member by which the victim can gauge his or her willingness to now be responsible. Usually sufficient plans and contingency plans can be made to protect the victim if the victimizer once again becomes destructive. Finally, giving the opportunity for compensation provides both the victim and the victimizer with another chance for a relationship with multiple opportunities. Not all the relational chips are placed in a once-and-for-all confrontation. Instead, relational issues are dealt with through a myriad of ways. Sometimes the relationship and interactions yield progress in love and trust issues, and sometimes they do not; but the players are able to continue pursuing the work of forgiveness because they know that the relational quality will be judged as a whole and not just on single productive or unproductive exchanges.

### Giving the Opportunity for Compensation and the Dimension of Relational Ethics

The dimension of relational ethics poses a difficult challenge to anyone who pursues forgiveness through giving the opportunity for compensation. In any family situation where forgiveness is necessary, the relational balance and justice in the family have been violated in a most severe way. People who have been hurt in this manner actually make decisions about the life and death of the relationship between them and their perpetrators. They have been innocent victims of a family crime against love and justice, which has damaged them and will damage their potential posterity. They have a *justified* claim against their perpetrator. A victim who gives the opportunity for compensation must relinquish the claim to this injustice and be willing to accept the effort of the wrongdoer to make the situation right.

This ability to give up one's justified claim to the injustice is very difficult to accomplish because it means going against the reality that exists in the emotional field of the family. My emotional field tells me that the person who has damaged me is indebted to me and should pay up. It also tells me that this violator has broken the law of justice and should be punished. There are people who have been damaged so severely by someone in their families that they truly believe that there is nothing the culprit could ever do to make the situation or the family better. In these situations, it is not that the victim demands total and immediate compensation for the undeserved violation, it is that the victim believes there is *no* adequate compensation for the violation. This was the case with a young woman who experienced the trauma of her intoxicated brother disfiguring her when he smashed a beer mug into her face.

> I know that it might be better for me if I would forgive him, but I can't. Every time I look in the mirror, every time I touch the side of my face, I remember what he did to me. I see that glass flying at my face. It wouldn't matter what he did or what I would do, I would always see that glass and that brings back all the hate I have for him and the way he has always treated me.

In cases such as these, the emotional trauma cannot be addressed through giving the opportunity for compensation. For instance, if the relationship improved between the brother and sister and the brother acted more responsibly, the sister would still be unable to give up the claim to the injustice. Responsible and trustworthy actions in the future would do nothing to adjust the sister's emotional claim to the damage already done. Compensation for the debt incurred is impossible.

In most cases, however, individuals are able to imagine how the person who used or abused them could make it up to them. Allowing for compensation does not mean that they cancel out the indebtedness of the victimizer; rather it means that they give up the claim to immediate and complete compensation. It means that they are willing to accept a "payment plan" from the wrongdoer concerning the tremendous debt that has been incurred because of the violation. Most often, these payment plans consist of opportunities or tests of trustworthiness for the violator. The plan may be explicit between the two parties, but most often is a criterion set forth only in the mind of the person who was an innocent victim. Such was the case of a young man who had been victimized by his mother through repeated acts of physical violence and who now had small children.

> It's hard, but every time my mother is with my children and enjoys them and treats them right, it makes me feel a little better. I still don't leave them alone with her, but I think that one day I might be able to. When she acts normal with my kids it makes me think that maybe she is starting to become normal.

In this instance, trust is tentative but is expressed as a potential. The implication is that if the mother continues to treat her grandchildren responsibly, then the son will be able to credit the mother as being more trustworthy and the relationship may one day be significantly improved. The son is the one willing to give up his claim to his mother's indebtedness and let her "work off" the obligation to him. Contrast this with the story of a young woman from a similar family situation who is unwilling to give up her claim to the injustice and give her mother the opportunity to compensate for the abuse.

> It infuriates me for my mother to be nice to them (the children). She's living a lie! She acts like this great grandmother—all loving—and she beat the hell out of me when I was a kid. Why didn't she do that stuff for me?

To give up claim to the injustice, the innocent victim of family harm must give to the victimizer. Victims give by providing a way for a normalized relationship between themselves and the victimizer. Regardless of the imbalance of give-and-take and the violation of trust between the two, victims must give in the sense of being willing to set the imbalance aside and allow *incremental* trust opportunities and exchanges in the relationship. This also requires victims to enter into the relationship ready to fulfill their obligations to the relationship. These may include meeting the needs of the victimizer, as was the case with a middle-aged woman who had been used and manipulated by her mother for most of her life.

> I have to tell myself every day not to focus on what my mom doesn't do for me. It used to be everything I did for her I resented her that much more, and so I would try to do less. When I expect her to do something for me and look at what she can do, it makes me feel better. When I know she is trying to meet my needs I feel better about doing things for her. It seems like when I don't resent her as much she tends to do a little more.

The work of forgiving in giving the opportunity for compensation is actually *fore-giving* on the part of the victim. The victim contributes to the relationship before the destructive trauma that caused the pain is addressed. This giving on the part of the victim should be incremental and gauged also as to be appropriate to the damaged status of the relationship and not overwhelm the victim or victimizer.

### Giving the Opportunity for Compensation and the Dimension of Family Transactions

Families make their power structures and belief systems overt by the way they engage in systemic transactions. As we have discussed earlier, these transactions or patterns can perpetuate destructive behavior and pain in the victim of unjust abuse or manipulation. The third station in the work of forgiveness is somewhat dependent upon changing these patterns and transactions so they can promote trustworthy instead of destructive behavior. In giving the opportunity for compensation, one must address three elements that are defined by the family transactions:

communication, hierarchy, and beliefs. Although these elements are intertwined in this dimension and to some degree define one another, it is helpful to analyze how some aspects of each affect the family transactions as a whole.

In families where there has been a severe violation of love and trust, there are two predominant communication patterns. First, many of these damaged families carry secrets about the unjustified violations. The dramatic thing about family secrets is that most everyone in the family knows the secret but refuses to communicate openly about it. The victim of an undeserved hurt can change this pattern by communicating openly about issues the family normally keeps under cover. This open communication need not directly involve the violation, but the open communication will have an effect on how the secret violation is handled. The story of a woman who was deeply hurt by her father's alcoholism is a case in point.

> Everybody would freeze up and not say a word when my father would drink. We would act like he wasn't drinking. When I finally said, "I think you have had enough because you can't stand up," he responded by saying that he would sleep it off. I didn't tell him how much his alcoholism had hurt me, but my saying something brought it out in the open. Now we can talk about it, and the whole family is now talking about it to him.

The second pattern of communication in damaged families is triangles. In other words, instead of talking directly to one another, two family members triangulate a third person in the relationship in order to communicate. Most often, triangles serve to diffuse and confuse communication patterns. Refusal to participate in triangles or commenting on the communication triangle is often enough to undo the pattern.

Almost all families have power hierarchies and coalitions that serve the family as a healthy function. Many times, however, these hierarchies and coalitions can perpetuate harmful transactions, as was the case with a woman who was sexually abused by her brothers.

> I was always so upset by it [the abuse] that I never could do anything in school. My brothers would treat me like I was dumb and make fun of me. I just got beat down further and further. They still make me feel that way.

Many times destructive hierarchies can be challenged directly or by forming other coalitions that are more powerful. This is essential if the work in the third station of forgiveness is to be accomplished. If not, the hierarchy will most likely continue to enact the same form of abuse that perpetuated the abuse in the beginning. Often the use of friends, spouses, or other family members as objective coalition members can assist the victim in finding strategies to change the power alignment in the family.

Powerful belief patterns are often formed by this dimension of family transactions. These beliefs turn into family rules that are sometimes very difficult to go against. Such was the case with a young man who felt his mother unfairly manipulated his life for her own gain.

> She is so oppressive. She made and makes me feel guilty for anything I ever wanted to do for myself. But she has had such a hard life and gave everything she had to make me a success. If I tell her how I feel, I will be an ingrate.

In this instance, the son has bought into the belief system the belief that the mother is all sacrificing and to express his own desire would make him an ungrateful son. Such belief perpetuation makes transactions in the third station of forgiveness difficult at best. Beliefs and family rules must be honestly challenged by the victim. Most often, the family or victimizer will resist such challenge, but the changed transaction will eventually promote trustworthy actions. For example, a wife who could not forgive her husband for physically abusing her was fearful of her husband's using her alcoholic past against her by telling her children. Although the husband was progressing and promised not to bring up the alcoholism, the wife's belief made her past a threat and she would not trust the husband. The therapist in the case suggested that she tell the children about the past herself. The wife was surprised to discover that the children were very accepting of her and were kind with regard to her past. This change in belief structure removed the threat of retribution from the husband, and she was much more willing to accept and trust his compensatory behavior.

## Giving the Opportunity for Compensation and the Dimension of Individual Psychology

During the Los Angeles riots of 1992 after the acquittal of the police officers seen on videotape beating Rodney King, the world was witness to the pent up anger and hostility that result from long-term injustice. The violence and rage of the city gave testimony to what happens when people feel that they are oppressed and cheated and there is no opportunity to set the injustice right. Of course the verdict in the trial of the officers who were accused of brutalizing King was not the only injustice; it was but one of the injustices perceived in a long string of imbalances that were racially slanted.

It is when there is no hope of justice or balance that people lose their faith in relationships. This hopelessness then drives a reasoning that states that the reality of justice does not matter. Victims of perpetual injustice feel that whatever happens in the future, they will end up being victimized again. They despair of the relationship ever being loving or trusting. Hopelessness then fuels extreme and absurd behaviors that are separated from well-reasoned reality. The facts are that when victims lose hope, they believe simply that whatever action is taken does not matter.

Separated from reality by a dramatic loss of hope, these individuals may take several courses of action against humanity or posterity. The action may be extremely passive or tragically aggressive, but both are equally destructive in that they detract from the reciprocal and responsible way of relating to others. The lack of hope victims feel produces a helter-skelter influence on their internal motivations toward love, power, and pleasure. When they give the opportunity for compensation, because of its gradual nature of testing the relational waters, it has the potential to make them once again hopeful. No matter how guarded this hopefulness is, it ties the individuals' psychological dimension back into the relational reality of justice and responsibility. This third station in the work of forgiveness, therefore, directs victims' internal motivations toward restoration and illuminates hope.

## Giving the Opportunity for Compensation and the Dimension of Facts

In giving the opportunity for compensation, victims must rely heavily on the facts as they present themselves in the here-and-now. Factual realities that have affected the family and relationships were subjected to little control in the past, but now are certainly beyond any effect the family may put forth. These past factual realities can hinder the process of addressing forgiveness in the here-and-now. Such was the case with the practical concern of a woman who was in desperate need of dentures and whose father offered to pay for the dental work.

> My father drank up every dime. I was grown before I saw a dentist or doctor because we had no money. Now my teeth are ruined! The way I see it, if he didn't care then I'm sure not going to let him take care of me now.

This woman saw her father's irresponsible acts as directly related to the facts she now experienced. No matter how justified her resentment was, as long as she allowed the past economic hardship and the corresponding result on her teeth to affect her regard for her father, she would not allow the father to compensate her in any way. The facts of the past had to be put aside to allow for the factual effort of the father in the here-and-now.

Many victims of unjust harm have trouble articulating just what the relational culprit can do to make compensation for the hurt. In this third station of forgiveness, the more specific and factual victims can be concerning their expectations of what they want from the wrongdoer, the more able the victims will be to judge the effort of the wrongdoer. For instance, if I want my victimizer to start showing me care or respect, he or she may or may not know what I mean. However, if I express a desire for them to help me with childcare, take me out for lunch, introduce me to his or her friends, or ask me questions about my life, the victimizer will have a clear idea of what to do and I will have a clear basis to judge whether I am receiving care and respect. The more clearly I make known the facts, the more I will receive in the way of compensation.

## GIVING THE OPPORTUNITY FOR COMPENSATION AND THE WORK OF FORGIVENESS

Some would question whether forgiveness is actually forgiveness at all if it is done over a period of time. After all, forgiving means giving up one's claim to the injustice and reestablishing the relationship based on love and trust. Can forgiveness be accomplished by degrees with no overt confrontation on the issue that violated another? I believe that in most cases forgiving is a process that is worked out over a long period of time. Humans are such that our memories and emotional status are usually changed, but the change occurs at a pace. It does not mean that there are not important watershed issues that are accomplished in the process, but the ethical, emotional, and interactional work connected with forgiveness is tied together.

Giving the opportunity for compensation involves the victim and victimizer in building a bridge to one another with only a rough idea of a plan. Once the decision is made to build, one will fasten one end of a girder and wait for the other to fasten the other end. If both work at it, then a structure is eventually built and reinforced, connecting the two in relationship. Some efforts in building are successful and some are not, but the commitment and the realism of effort to connect with one another are strong enough to explore new relationship strategies and tolerate mistakes when those strategies do not work. Each mutual effort brings the two closer together and further from the violation of love and trust. In this manner, forgiveness is accomplished over a period of time.

Whether or not the victim and victimizer know specifically the actions and interactions that produced the injustice, both almost always know the relational status between the two. Both live with the reality that the undeserved hurt has caused separation. It is not the talk about the issue that is the work of forgiveness but the closing of the gap between the two and the reestablishment of the relationship. Violation and lack of trust from the past fade in the presence of love and trust in the present. Therefore, I believe that forgiveness can be accomplished, even if the two parties do not talk overtly about the undeserved hurts in the past.

*Chapter Five*

# STATION FOUR: THE OVERT ACT OF FORGIVENESS

One of the memories that hopefully is etched into my brain permanently is the wonder I felt at the birth of my first child. I remember holding my little girl in my arms only a few hours after she had been born and my wife resting at my side in a silent, subdued room. I was filled with such wonder because of the thought that this new little one was the physical representation of the intimacy that my wife and I shared. Genetically she is half of me and half of my wife. Not that she is guaranteed to get the best part of either of us, but she is testimony to our struggle to bind ourselves together. Such intimacy requires not only commitment but also humility as we lose a little bit of ourselves in the relationship to gain what the other has to offer. But even more wondrous than my daughter being the representation of our intimacy was the fact that she was a brand new, different person. Perfect. In that one moment my daughter seemed unscathed by life and full of potential to do anything.

It is a great thing about relationships that what we have between ourselves and other people is more than the compilation of our parts. When we engage in a relationship, an invisible bond is formed that has a personality and being of its own. In essence, an invisible person called "us" is created in the union that is not quite like either person. It is a unique birth experience between humans that have an intimate relationship. The "us" is made up of parts of both me and you, but the bond between transcends either of us.

The sustenance that keeps this transcendent bond of "us" alive is the invisible attributes of love, justice, and trust that are maintained. Essentially, I am able to a sacrifice myself because I care for you and trust you to give me access to you. Denying access to these attributes absolutely detracts from the relationship and makes "us" weaker. There are, however, violent assaults to love, justice, and trust that not only make the relationship weaker, but can actually kill the relationship. When I experience undeserved hurt that insults my extension of love and trust, sacrifice of myself for the sake of "us" is no longer feasible or possible. Therefore, a choice is made: I participate in the destruction or murder of "us" in order to salvage myself.

It is in such relational trauma that the work of forgiveness is so powerful. Whatever the violence or abuse, persons in the relationship have experienced undeserved hurts to the point where the transcendent bond of "us" has had to be put to death. The work of forgiveness as described up to this point in insight, understanding, and giving the opportunity for compensation is designed to either mourn the death of the relationship and move on, or to revive the relationship in a gradual and sequential manner. Time and the combination of insight, understanding, and giving the opportunity for compensation may indeed result in heartfelt forgiveness. However, the fourth station of forgiveness, *the overt act of forgiveness,* is much more sudden and dramatic. In essence, the overt act of forgiveness is like a relational rebirthing. The two relational partners breathe life into their bond of "us" and mutually pledge to love and trust in the relationship in a responsible manner much in the same way that new parents respond to a newborn. Instead of reviving the old relationship, the overt act of forgiving is like smacking the behind of a new "us" life.

## FAMILIES AND FORGIVENESS

The gravity of violations of love and trust in families can be profound. Some violations that cause pain are extremely covert: a divorced parent's using a child's welfare or loyalty to retaliate or inflict damage on a former spouse; an addict's requiring a family sacrifice to shoulder a burden to enable the addict to look good; or a parent's using a child to fulfill his or her frustrated ambitions for success or glory. Other painful family violations are extraordinarily overt in the insult to fairness: a family member's viciously abusing another; a parent's refusing to give a child essential food, water, or care; or violent acts or threats of violent acts such as suicide or murder. These are just some of the reasons that family members become so damaged that they feel they must put an end to the relationship. Pain and risk become too overwhelming to tolerate relational closeness.

Family members have different perspectives on these violations, but the entire family knows that there is something desperately wrong. As we have seen before, a parent of an unjustly abused child may feel entitled to take the destructive action because he or she may have been abused or victimized in a similar fashion. However, even the abusive individual who feels entitled to a destructive action knows the ramifications such actions have on family relationships. I believed my mother was abusive to me. On the other hand, she believed that she was a good and sacrificing parent who deserved obedient and caring children. But she and I both knew that the family was void of loving and trusting attributes that forced distance in the family and eventually put relationships at risk.

## Responsibility for Relational Deterioration

It is often difficult to sort out the responsibility of the victim who has now turned to victimizing an innocent family member. The following excerpt is from a young medical student who was abused by his father. When we hear his story, we see how the young man's father is responsible for vicious acts.

> From as far back as I can remember, my father demanded that I maintain perfect grades. He would constantly berate me for my classroom performance telling me that I would never amount to anything. He literally cut me off. He padlocked my door nightly to make sure I would study. When I did what he considered substandard work, he would go nuts. He would threaten to kill me—one time he almost busted my jaw because I made a "B" on a test.

Common sense tells us that the father is indeed responsible for unreasonable abuse of his son. His responsibility for violation seems clear until we hear his story.

> My family was poor and I never had any opportunity. I only saw my father once in my life and then he was drunk and passed out on the floor. He never helped us once. I had to work every day of my life to keep our family afloat. My mother had to have help so I did what I had to do to make money. I never once had a job that I enjoyed. I've always had to do some job where some guy who thought he was better than me told me what to do. I swore to myself that my son would have the opportunities that I didn't have. I know that I am hard on him, but he's not having to work near as hard as I did. Besides, it is good for him to learn the value of hard work that will pay off. When he has made something of himself, he can do as he pleases. But as long as I pay the bills, he owes it to me to do as I say.

The three-generation context of family violations makes responsibility for the violation difficult to ascertain. Is it fair to hold this father responsible for the abuse of his son when his reason for doing so is so clearly tied to the victimization he experienced? Should he shoulder the blame alone for the abuse of his son?

As much as we might understand the father's background and how it contributed to his destructive action, he is fully responsible. In essence, the father was innocently victimized and to maintain a legitimate sense of self, he victimized another innocent party. In reality, however, the injustice and the violation the father experienced should have been forced back to his relationship with his own father. In closing off the relationship, the father participated in killing off the bond between him and his father. Instead of the guilt being placed where it belonged, the father transferred the ramifications for the guilt to his son. Therefore, a victimizer who has been victimized by family is responsible for participating in the doing away with a harmful relationship and transferring the guilt and obligation of that relationship to an innocent party.

The injustices and violations of love and trust in families seldom originate with just one person at a point in time. Most often they are passed through the three-generational complex. But each generation is responsible to hold the relationships intact. In this manner, guilt for violations is placed in the context of the relationships where the violations were received. Keeping these relationships intact does not necessarily mean that one must have continuing contact with or exposure to a wrongdoer. As we have discussed, the relationship with even an irresponsible destructive family member can be dealt with using elements of insight and understanding. However, the victim of destructive action must continue to hold the violations in the relationships to which they belong. Failure to do so means that the victim becomes responsible for future victimization.

The father in the above case, however, is not totally the culprit for the awful abusive effects. The entire lineage of the family has contributed to the deterioration of love and trust that now currently plays itself out between the father and son. Even as abusive as the father is, his intentions for the son have some elements of care. In other words, the father's intentions are not to do the son harm, but to do better for the son. His methodology is twisted and unsound, but he is not culpable for lack of care. The blame for the deterioration in love and trust is not his alone, even though he is responsible for the current violations.

The father's failure to keep his violation in the relationship where it belongs makes him responsible for his destructive action toward his son. However, the son also is responsible for the justified balance of give-and-take in the relationship with the father. If the son kills off the relationship with his father, he is also responsible for destructive action that will seal into him the violation of love and trust he received from his father. The son, who is currently a victim, in turn becomes the potential victimizer as he will most likely transfer the father's guilt and retribution for the guilt to an innocent party. In other words, victims are still responsible for maintaining the existence of relationships even when they have been violated. If I am an innocent victim of destructive action from my family, I am not excused from exercising relational responsibility. I am not entitled to retaliation for the injustice in any way and I am still obligated to my responsibility to exercise a balance of give-and-take relationships. If I, as a victim, retaliate or throw off the guilt of my victimizer onto someone else, I too am responsible for the murder of the bond between "us" and further contribute to the deterioration of love and trust in the family.

## For the Sake of "Us"

Both the victim and the victimizer in a family have a stake in making the relationship between them right. The victimizer has inflicted on an innocent person some destructive action for which amends must be made. The victim can justly fulfill future obligations to the family relationship only if the guilt and responsibility for the violations are rectified in the relational context in which the damage occurred. This is what makes the work of forgiveness perhaps the supreme manifestation of family relationships. It always involves the work of at least two people willing to rebuild love and trust between them even after severe damage. This work not only gives the victim and victimizer what they need as individuals, it also provides the family posterity with the cleanest slate possible. Love and trust are restored in the intergenerational family because love and trust are restored in the "us" relationship from which posterity will come.

Because both relational parties have a vested interest and responsibility, the process of forgiving may be initiated from either. Whether there occurs reestablishment through giving the opportunity for compensation or rebirthing by the overt act of forgiveness, the bond is forged through mutual cooperation and trust in spite of the damaged relationship. The process of forgiving cannot be accomplished alone. Just as both parties know when there is a vacuum of love and trust in the family, both are partners in the knowledge of restoration of relational security.

## Forgiveness with Integrity

In order for forgiving to be effective in this restoration, both parties must have integrity about the process. Both must accept the other as genuine about the effort to put the relationship back together. The innocent party and the wrongdoer must see one another as valued members of the family and honestly deal with the destructive harm that was perpetuated between them. Most importantly, both must make the effort in their transactions to have a balance of entitlements and obligations.

Without this integrity in the process of forgiving, more relational damage is done. If either party sees access to the relationship as opportunity for self-justification or retribution, the relationship will deteriorate. Many use a disguise of forgiveness in order to gain a hearing for their own pain or damage or to inflict damage on the other. This was the case with a woman who was "forgiving" her husband for an affair.

> I forgive you for causing me so much pain. You have made me feel worthless. You have taken everything that I am and made me nothing. It was your choice and I will always know how you thought about our marriage. But I will not allow you to hurt me that way anymore, so I will forgive you.

This woman, who was in deep pain, was not engaged in forgiving. She was using the process to plead her case of rage against her husband. Not only was she unwilling to release the damage caused by the husband's violation, she was also unwilling to accept any future effort on the husband's part to restore the relationship. Unfortunately, these types of interchanges only confuse the issue of forgiveness and contribute to the instability of love and trust between family members.

The work of forgiveness in families is far from perfect. Even when both parties approach the process with integrity and the best intentions, many times there is remaining emotional baggage from the relational transgression that is difficult to slough off. The following is a report from a man who had been abused by his father and had worked through the relationship to the point of forgiveness.

> I was watching a movie where a boy was sexually abused. Suddenly I felt all the shame and anger that I hadn't felt for years. The pain was incredible. It's so confusing. My father is a changed man who is really loving and nurturing. I have a good relationship with him. But since the film, I have had to remind myself that the issue that I had with him has been taken care of. I have forgiven him, but I've been bitten by this depression and anger from the past.

Forgiving family members for past violations does not guarantee that we forget the pain that is associated with the destructive behavior. Sights, sounds, touches, and even smells and tastes can propel us back to feelings and memories of unfortunate occurrences in the family. So the process of forgiving is neither static nor once for all. It is a confusing, oscillating process that moves us between stations of forgiveness and the past that makes us want to give up on the family.

## THE OVERT ACT OF FORGIVING

There have been moments in history when the words of one person have been able to penetrate the hearts of others to foster great compassion, commitment, and courage. Winston Churchill inspired his compatriots with his "their finest hour" speech. John Kennedy rallied a new generation to global interaction in his "The torch is passed" inaugural address. Even though Lincoln's Gettysburg address was given a mediocre reception initially, people soon realized that he was speaking for the ages. In the time and space framework in which we exist, humans can be persuaded and inspired to bind together for great causes or actions.

The fourth station in the work of forgiveness is *the overt act of forgiving*. This fourth station is unique in the work of forgiveness because it focuses immense effort and importance on one point in time in the lives of the innocent victim of family violation and the perpetrator of the violation. Many times overtly bringing up the subject of forgiving between two people is the culmination of much time and groundwork that has accumulated enough of a baseline of love and trust to enable direct discussion of damage. Other times, the overt act of forgiving serves as a kick start to a damaged relationship where the elements of love and trust can be constructed in the future. In the first case, overt forgiving is built on the sound structure of the relational bridge that the victim and victimizer have constructed between them. Overt forgiving in this case is simply a sealing of the agreement between the two parties that they are now different in the way they relate in a trustworthy fashion and the past is resolved.  In the second case, the reconnection may be makeshift and temporary as a bridge is facilitated between the two, but will have to be reinforced by time and the steady and trustworthy interchanges of the future.  But in either case, direct confrontation of family pain that has violated individuals is one of the moments in the family history that can enable and facilitate acts of compassion, courage, and commitment between family members.

When the opportunity for compensation is given, forgiveness is achieved a little at a time over a long period of time as the victimizer proves to the victim that the relationship can now be trusted.  However, the overt act of forgiving differs in that forgiveness is achieved by the positioning of the victim and victimizer in an immediate alignment of love and trust.  Instead of the victim's prescribing a payment plan designed to gradually erase the indebtedness of the victimizer who caused the pain, the victim essentially cancels out any claim to the injustice.  In discussing the violation and forgiveness openly and overtly, the innocent person and the wrongdoer come to an agreement that they will have the freedom to relate to one another in a new way—unhindered by the damaged past and its implications for obligations and entitlements in the relationship.

This overt act of forgiving does not necessarily preclude a backwash of emotional turmoil such as defensiveness or anger. Many times the overt act of forgiveness is just the beginning point for those in a damaged family relationship to learn how to address and work out the hurts of the past.  But the point in time where the pain is addressed and forgiveness is facilitated dictates a sudden and new intent and form of relationship for the victim and victimizer. The overt act of forgiveness represents a new covenant or contract in the balance of give-and-take between the two parties.  In order to make this new covenant or contract a reality between the innocent party and the perpetrator, at least three distinct elements concerning the past must be achieved.

## Agreement

It does not matter if the wrongdoer or the wronged person initiates the subject of the past violation; both must come to an agreement concerning the specifics of the violation. If one party or the other denies or does not remember specific important details of the destructive action that caused pain, many times there will be a question of reliability between the two. For instance, a young man reeled under the burden of having his father tell him that he was ashamed of him because of his misbehavior. The event, for the young man, crystallized his beliefs about his father's attitude toward him. However, the father never remembered the incident and stated that he would have never said such a thing to his son. The lack of agreement between the two made a direct discussion of forgiveness extremely difficult.

Agreement between the victim and the victimizer on the details surrounding the violation need not be absolute. Many times individuals will forget important details or simply block unpleasant memories. For there to be agreement, both must recognize that a severe and meaningful violation transpired between them.

## Acknowledgment

After agreement has been conceded between the two persons concerning some specifics of the violation, acknowledgment of responsibility for the hurt and pain the violation caused must be made. Acknowledgment of this responsibility on the part of the wrongdoer is a crucial aspect in facilitating the victim's ability to cancel a claim on the injustice. In essence, when the victimizer acknowledges having unjustly damaged a family member, he or she takes a position of self-accountability. The self-accountability gives the victim reassurance that justice will be served in the future.

## Apology

At some point in the overt act of forgiveness, there has to be some apology for the damage that has been perpetrated. The apology serves a twofold purpose. First, it overtly states to the victim that the victimizer would desire to erase the pain if possible. In essence, if the victimizer could live the situation in which the violation was perpetrated again, he or she would rectify the damage. Second, it at least covertly serves as a promise to the victim that the victimizer regrets the past and will try to interact in a loving and trustworthy manner in the future. Therefore, apology serves both the victim and the victimizer as a method or promise of restitution for the injustices of the past.

Included in this apology must be recognition of the new intent for and status of the relationship. This is accomplished by both the victim and the victimizer. The apology of the wrongdoer has no effect if the victim of the damage refuses to accept the apology. As long as the victim retains the violation as an incorrectable injustice, the relationship will be fractured. Therefore, the apology must include the dynamic of the victim's accepting the apology and releasing the claim of the injustice. In short, the victim must also forgive. In return, the victimizer must accept the gesture of forgiveness as a sign that the relationship can pursue a balanced and justified give-and-take. If the victimizer apologizes but refuses to accept the forgiveness, he or she will withdraw from the relationship in either a defensive or self-degrading posture.

## Overt Forgiving and the Dimension of Relational Ethics

One of the amazing things about the democracy of the United States is the smooth transition of power in our executive branch. Once every four years on January 20, we transfer power from one president to the next. Even when changes are unexpected, such as with the resignation of Richard Nixon, we as citizens accept the transfer of power in a stable manner. Not one former president has ever refused to leave office or used political and military strength to challenge the right of the next elected president to take office. Transition is smooth and expected. Therefore, former presidents become ordinary citizens with a very nice pension. They have no more control over the powerful resources of the nation than you or I. The power and *responsibility* belong to another person.

When there is unjustified violation of an innocent family member by another, the damage gives the victim a justified claim against the perpetrator. The victim was either denied the care and nurturing to which he or she was justifiably entitled or forced to fulfill inappropriate obligations by another or both. The resulting damage and hurt that a victim feels after being violated by a family member—if he or she is to satisfy the innate sense of fairness—put the victim in the position to hold the victimizer responsible for the injustice. In other words, the victim holds the victimizer accountable for his or her actions. The transgressed must hold the transgressor accountable until justice is done.

In the fourth station of forgiveness, the responsibility and accountability for the relational damage are not forgotten or obliterated from existence. Justice demands compensation or restitution; therefore, prior violations of obligations cannot be wished out of existence. However, the overt act of forgiveness does change the status of relational ethics between the victim and victimizer in that the accountability and responsibility for the damage are transferred. When both parties come to an agreement on the violation and the victimizer acknowledges responsibility and apologizes, the victim can release the charge of the relationship. No longer does the forgiver have to hold the forgiven wrongdoer responsible or accountable for the injustice; the forgiven person holds himself or herself responsible. This forgiveness in an overt fashion can have tremendous restorative and healing power to not only the relationship but also the individuals. The following is a report from a middle-aged woman who overtly discussed her childhood with her abusive mother.

> I told her about a few of the incidents that I remembered.
> She remembered some and some she did not. But she said
> that she knew that she was out of control and that she was
> sure that what I said was true. Then she held me close and
> said, "I always have loved you and I am sorry I did not
> show it." All the hate and anger I had inside collapsed. I
> held on tight to her and bawled like a baby. I just knew
> that everything was going to be okay.

Overt confrontation of the past damage and violation between
family members has an immediate effect on the relationship, but
it does not set the past right. Only when the forgiven person
responsibly executes his or her obligation to care for and nurture
the innocent party is the burden for past destructive actions
rectified. Therefore, the overt act of forgiving has a dynamic
effect in beginning a fair relationship, but is effective only as the
relational members seek to be loving and trustworthy with each
other in the future.

It is hardly unusual for a person who has been innocently
victimized by a family member to retaliate against the victimizer
in a likewise unjustified manner. When family members engage
in the overt act of forgiving, it is very common for the "victim"
to recognize his or her relational irresponsibility toward the
"victimizer." When the violator accepts responsibility for his or
her damaging actions and apologizes, the shift in the relational
ethics dimension no longer gives the violated party access to
justification of his or her own destructive behavior. Recognition
of the victim's self-justifying retaliation often becomes immediately apparent when the victimizer shifts the ethical balance by
taking responsibility, as was the case with an elderly woman who
was lied to by her daughter.

> My daughter had hardly gotten the words "forgive me" out
> of her mouth before I was apologizing for the way that I
> had treated her. I called her awful names and I've done
> a lot of things that I shouldn't have.

In many of these cases, the roles of forgiver and forgiven oscillate between the relational parties. Because one member takes responsibility for destructive action, the other takes appropriate responsibility. Therefore, the overt act of forgiving sets the ethical responsibility in the dimension right, and it serves as a stabilizing force between the members as they try to maintain a balanced relationship in the future and guard against future damage.

## Overt Forgiving and the Dimension of Family Transactions

Forgiving is serious business. The words of forgiveness are very easy to say and are often tossed around without forgiveness actually being achieved. It is possible for family members to maintain the same patterns, hierarchies, and belief systems that perpetuated family violation while speaking the words of apology or forgiveness. Such transactions entrench the relational dimension, and no change in relationship is facilitated between the victim and the wrongdoer. For instance, the following transaction took place between a mother and daughter in a therapy session.

DAUGHTER: The things that you have done and said in the past have hurt.

MOTHER: Well we can't judge the hearts of others. If I have hurt you, then I am sorry. I let the past be the past.

DAUGHTER: But it is the past that keeps coming up that continues to do the damage.

MOTHER: So forgive me for it and let the past go.

In this interchange, the mother had apologized and asked for forgiveness, but nothing in the relationship had changed. The mother was still in a powerful and domineering position, and the daughter was still left with the burden for the relational injustice.

In order to facilitate a change in the dimension of family

transactions and to ensure that the work of forgiveness is realized, I have found it helpful to have the family perform rituals around the overt act of forgiving. The power of rituals in families has been discussed in several places (e.g., Kobak & Waters, 1984; Imber-Black, 1988a; Imber-Black, 1988b). In the action of family healing, the family transaction performed in the ritual has the capability and the power to break old patterns and rules and transcend the interaction into a powerful relational reality.

In the fourth station of forgiveness, I primarily suggest rituals to heighten the family experience of agreement, acknowledgment, or apology. The particular forgiveness ritual that the family performs will differ from situation to situation. It is important to remember that the ritual, when utilized, must be important to both the forgiver and the forgiven. In situations where there has been a severe family violation but much time has passed since the injustice, I have suggested that the two relational parties work out as much specific detail of the violation as possible and then choose items that represent the trauma. When these items are present to the victim and the victimizer, it brings the situation closer to both and agreement on the injustice is easier. In the following case, a wife had an affair and was asking forgiveness from her husband. After discussion of the affair, the wife was asked to present something that would represent the affair. At the next session, the wife brought a shirt she had kept from the other man.

WIFE:        I guess I was holding onto this for a reason. I
             wasn't quite ready to let you know everything
             about him.
HUSBAND:  What was it?
WIFE:        Even though you knew about the affair, I still
             wanted to hold onto some of the feelings for him.
             The affair was wrong, but I think I was going to
             try to keep part of the affair emotionally. I guess
             that is why I kept the shirt. I'm ready to give
             that part of it up now.

Many people will use pictures, photographs, mementos, toys, or a variety of other objects to help them reckon with the impact of the injustice and the transgression.

Many times when the two relational parties start working on the overt act of forgiveness, the victimizer will have difficulty with understanding and therefore acknowledging the damage done by the injustice. This can be for a variety of reasons, but sometimes it is simply because time has faded many unpleasant memories. This in turn can make it difficult for the victim to believe the apology of the victimizer because the victim does not feel the hurt has been responsibly handled. In some of these situations, I have suggested rituals that show brokenness and contriteness on the part of the victimizer. These assist the victimizer to reckon with the gravity of the transgression and clearly demonstrate to the victim that the wrongdoer is serious about forgiveness. In one such case, a man was asked to perform a ritual symbolizing his belief that he understood the pain he caused the wife when he physically abused her. At the next session, the man wore a flat bicycle innertube around his neck.

HUSBAND: I felt like by venting all my anger on her, I was as worthless as a flat. I hindered the marriage. So I have decided that I would wear this for a month. When people ask me about it, I tell them that I want my wife and other people to know that I haven't treated my wife like I should.

WIFE: I want to tell you something. I was embarrassed at first, but the longer you wore that thing the better I felt. It showed me you were really sorry.

Some people will shave their heads, rend their clothes, or wear sackcloth under their garments as a sign that they acknowledge the damage done to another family member. One ritual that I have utilized quite often is for the overt act of forgiveness to take place with the victimizer on his or her knees. This action, although quite simple, greatly affects the emotional realm of both victim and victimizer and usually changes the transactions tremendously because the participants are so unfamiliar with the action. Madanes (1991) has utilized this transaction in a strategic manner to deal with a sex offender apologizing to the victim. Although some believe that the action is humiliating (Pettle, 1992) and places the victim in a one-up position, the ritual as I use it is designed simply to heighten the impact of the overt act. I exercise much care in trying to make sure that the victim identifies with the victimizer enough that a one-up, one-down transaction is avoided. This does not lessen the impact or the required humility needed to perform a ritual. Indeed, asking for and receiving forgiveness is extremely humbling. However, I find that most victims feel the humility with just as great an impact as the victimizers, as seen in the case with a middle-aged woman asking forgiveness for abusing her teenage daughter.

DAUGHTER: I don't want you on your knees. It makes me feel
          bad for you.
MOTHER:   It's the right place for me to be. It makes me feel
          right when I say I'm sorry.
DAUGHTER: I know, but I know how hard it is and I hurt.

Imagine how different the interaction between the mother and daughter in the first example in this section might have been had the mother been on her knees when apologizing and asking forgiveness. Chances are that the words would have been more difficult to say because their meanings would have been heightened to the point of reality for both mother and daughter. It is my experience that rituals, regardless of design, undo powerful family patterns and make the overt act of forgiveness more meaningful.

## Overt Forgiving and
## the Dimension of Individual Psychology

Much of the pain experienced by individuals in families is so burdening that every aspect of the person's psyche and internal processing is affected. When the violation is kept internal, victims will many times question the validity of their feelings. Did the violation occur? Am I making it out to be worse than it actually was? Am I using the abuse or manipulation as an excuse? These are just a few of the many questions that victims ask themselves.

The overt act of forgiving is very powerful in this dimension because it has the potential of providing victims with *validation* for their perspective of the event. When victims have the injustice confirmed overtly, they experience the act as support for their identity. Misconceptions about the injustice can be addressed and/ or vague recollections can be clarified. This support for the victims' perspective raises the victims' self-concept and allows them to be more confident. This was the case of a woman who had been sexually abused by her father but had never told anyone in the family about the violation. When she spoke to her father for the first time in years, she did not address the abuse directly but asked about the father's desertion.

> He told me that he did many things to me and that it was painful for him to remember the past. He said that he knew that was no excuse. Finally, I know I'm not crazy. What happened to me really did happen.

The overt act of forgiving can be essential in lifting a heavy burden of guilt—not only for the victim but also for the victimizer. Many times, victimizers have reeled for many years, knowing that they did great harm to a family member but not knowing how to address the situation. When the violation is handled overtly, the victimizer often feels a release and an ability to perform more responsibly in the relationship. Such was the case of a brother who had sexually abused his younger sister and had continued to be irresponsible in the relationship.

> I never felt like I could face her. When the family would get together, I would avoid her and her family. When I finally told her I was sorry for what I did to her, it made me feel like I could speak to her again. I can't change the past, but I can sure make some things up to her.

The vulnerability that overt forgiving requires seems to strengthen the individual psyches of both victim and victimizer. Although there may be several explanations for this phenomenon, one of the reasons is that people find more internal congruence if they deal with the truth. Even if that truth is unpleasant, internal mechanisms to reconcile self with reality are much more effective than defense mechanisms such as repression, projection, or rationalization. When relational parties are at their most vulnerable, they are often at their strongest.

## Overt Forgiving and the Dimension of Facts

The fourth dimension in the work of forgiveness, in the way that it reshapes the relational ethics dimension and family transactions, opens the door to the family for considerable change in the factual dimension. Of course, the past damage is part of the family history. However, many family members who engage in the overt act of forgiving and are successful in creating a new relationship go to great lengths to secure a healthier factual reality in the family for both themselves and their posterity. For example, the following is a description from a man who was physically abused by his family and had flown across the country to overtly discuss forgiveness.

> They didn't do everything perfect, but they did stay in the room with me. After we talked, I felt that they were more

nurturing to me than they had ever been. By the second day, I began to long for the day when I would trust my folks to be grandparents to my kids. On the last day there, I told this to them. They said they would be willing to move to where I live. I never really knew my grandparents. I don't know if I want them to move yet, but I think this might be a way that both of us can work together to make things better for my kids.

## THE OVERT ACT OF FORGIVING AND THE WORK OF FORGIVENESS

Many experience the overt act of forgiving as essential because it puts the relational injustice and violation to bed once and for all. Indeed, in many cases the overt act of forgiveness binds family members together in a new relationship that is much closer than the one they had before the damage occurred. However, negotiation of the interaction that includes the three elements of agreement, acknowledgment, and apology can be treacherous and opens up many opportunities for relational deterioration. The interchange between victim and victimizer may result in defensiveness, accusations, and counteraccusations. With all the positive potential that the overt act of forgiving has in relationships, it can also seal in destructive entitlement in both the victim and the victimizer.

Many consider the discomfort level and potential relational deterioration too threatening to pursue the overt act of forgiving. This is not only understandable, but in many cases wise. Overt forgiving is not appropriate in all situations and is certainly not for everyone. However, many others feel they cannot make relational progress until the injustice or violation is dealt with directly. There are several reasons that people give for this belief. First, some victims feel that they never can consider putting themselves in a position to have a relationship with a former victimizer until the victimizer understands the past and takes responsibility. In these cases, overt forgiving provides an initial rejunction that provides the victim with the trust and protection needed to continue a relationship.

Second, some victims feel that any future relationship they have with a person who did them harm must be based on honesty. Many believe that if they do not handle everything up front with the victimizer, then the relationship will have a "false feel" and will be built on faulty assumptions. Finally, some victims feel that anything short of the overt act of forgiving will be ineffective in healing a damaged relationship. In these situations, agreement about the violation, acknowledgment of responsibility for damage, and apology for hurt and promise of future trustworthiness by the victimizer are the only criteria by which the victim will accept a new relational reality from the one who has caused damage.

Even where the overt act of forgiving is considered absolutely essential to the work of forgiveness, it should be stressed that the parties need to confront the issues in the exchange but that the exchange need not be confrontational. Where overt forgiving works best, it is based on both the victim and the victimizer responsibly executing a balance of giving and receiving insight, understanding, and care from one another. Forgiving should not be placed into situations where there are two outs in the bottom of the ninth and someone has to hit a home run to save the relationship. In most cases, success in the overt act of forgiving is not achieved in a last desperate attempt by either party to make the relationship right. Such situations place enormous pressure on an already difficult situation.

Most often, the overt act of forgiving is successful when the victim and victimizer use the opportunity in such a way that it processes and develops elements from the other three stations of forgiveness. In this manner, the overt act of forgiving gives both the victim and the victimizer the opportunity to demonstrate their love and trust for one another while the work of forgiveness is being accomplished.

# Section Two

# The Work of Forgiveness in Therapy

*Chapter Six*

# HELPING FAMILY MEMBERS FORGIVE ONE ANOTHER

W hether we identify with a constructivist or an objectivist view, relationships serve as an anchor in our experience of reality. Relationships are like a cable that runs through the whole of life and are at one time our connection to the past and the future. We experience the complex threads of the cable of intertwined relationships in something called the here-and-now even though it clearly is tied to forgotten and vague recollections in the past and runs to a speculative and unclear future. But even though the pathway of the relationship cable is not clearly seen by us, we know that it is connected. The past relationships of our previous generations as well as our experiences with our friends and families clearly affect us in our here-and-now relational experiences. In the same manner, the relationship decisions we now make contribute to cable strength or weakness in the future. Changes in the relational structure now no doubt impact on and determine the relationships that we have in the future and in many ways affect our unborn lineage.

Like any person, a therapist helping a family or individual cannot know exactly where the cable had its origins and where it will end its journey. All the therapist sees in the here-and-now are the relational cables' strengths and damages. In these perplexing relational ties that are damaged, desire sometimes dictates that the relationship be severed. But our knowledge of the past and future implications of present relationships rightly leads us to caution. Certainly there are just causes for severing family relationships, and sometimes it is the only option. But in general, the severing of any family relationship weakens the future strength of the cable. In the same manner, any relational strand that can be repaired and strengthened in the here-and-now will contribute to the relational resources in the future.

The therapist sees the individual and family from an outside perspective that they can never have and has special knowledge of the relationships and life course to which the family is bound. With this perspective, the therapist has an essential job in the therapeutic work of forgiveness. The therapist's suggestions, pace, advice, and encouragement can gently move the individual or family members to the place that enables them to make the best judgments and decisions concerning the work of forgiveness. In enhancing the objectivity of the family members and helping them know the conditions, the therapist engages the family in the therapeutic work of forgiveness.

## THE GOALS AND PACE OF THERAPY

When there has been a serious violation in the family that makes the work of forgiveness necessary, it can be extremely confusing to both the therapist and the individuals in the family. Love and trust that are necessary for strong self-esteem and self-concept are locked into the context of relationships and are probably most powerfully demonstrated or refuted in family relationships. We may try to protect ourselves and our sense of individuality from dangerous and damaging family relationships only to find out that the love and trust we need for that healthy sense of self are in relationships. Most of the time, the integrity and protection of the self and the health and strength of relationships are tied together.

Family therapists have long noted that this ability to balance the needs and drives associated with autonomy and togetherness simultaneously is one of the primary keys to not only healthy individuals, but also healthy relationships. Bowen (1978) perhaps clarified this the best when he described this ability to balance individual/togetherness needs in degree of *differentiation*. The less a person is differentiated, the more anxiety he or she will feel as a result of the struggle to resolve identity and relationships. This anxiety will move less differentiated persons to extremes of distance and cutting themselves off from people or overinvolvement in relationships.

Distancing and cutoffs create a sort of pseudoindividual, as the person does not choose to be alone but rather seeks separateness out of anxiety about relationships. This type of behavior by individuals is often demonstrated by their perfectionistic, invulnerable, arrogant, and insensitive attitudes. On the other hand, overinvolvement in relationships creates a pseudointimacy as individuals overfunction and fuse their emotional field with another in order to avoid the anxiety that is a result of burdensome insecurity. This type of pseudointimacy is sometimes found in individuals who are chaotic, too vulnerable, and characterized by a severe lack of self-esteem.

True differentiation, or the ability to balance the needs and drives of individuality and togetherness, is difficult for any person to achieve. However, the task becomes increasingly unmanageable as individuals are damaged by family relationships. Still, the best hope for the individuals on their own and in their current and intergenerational relationships lies in their ability to be distinct individuals with clear boundaries who choose to give of themselves to relational intimacy. The goal of the therapeutic work of forgiveness is to work both ways, toward individuals and their relationships. The four stations of forgiveness are intended to protect, salvage, nurture, and restore as much of the individuals' self-esteem and integrity and as much of their current and individual relationships as possible.

It is essential that the therapist understand the mutuality of the individuals' contribution to the relationship and the relationship to the individuals. People who have been damaged in family relationships are still in need of the basic elements of love and trust, which serve as their anchors to reality. In my opinion, it is inappropriate for the therapist to guide a client to sacrifice family relationships for the client's sake or sacrifice the client's self for the sake of family relationships. Even when the therapist is working with only one individual who has been damaged by the intergenerational family, the intergenerational and relational context of the individual must always be kept in the forefront of the therapeutic work. The client has an essential role in healing the family, and the family has an essential role in healing the client. Therefore, the therapist must always be an advocate for both in a balanced fashion.

As previously mentioned, the work of forgiveness usually is attained a little at a time over a long period of time. This fits well with the individual/togetherness paradigm. As the individual gains insight and understanding into the intergenerational family and trust is built through compensatory and responsible relationships, the individual is likely to feel more love and security. As this love and security contribute to a stronger sense of self, the individual is then able to contribute and be trustworthy when considering current and intergenerational relationships. Therefore, the work of forgiveness in therapy is often on a slow gradient of growth that contributes to the individual and the family in an oscillating fashion.

One of the characteristics of intergenerational family therapy that is difficult to master is the continuing power of the past. Violation of love and trust in the intergenerational past is played out by individuals again and again in the same and slightly different ways with an array of relationships. The past of an individual who has been unjustly damaged in the past not only touches one point in time of the individual, it potentially touches every aspect of the individual's life. Therefore, the work of forgiveness in redressing the intergenerational past damage is seldom a once-and-for-all insight or resolution. It is work most often done in pieces. Healing work that an individual will accomplish in insight and understanding will often be challenged as current actions by the family defy understanding or unpleasant memories of the past are triggered in the context of a current relationship. Even when there is tremendous healing in the individual and the family, forgiveness is often like a receding tide in its effect on the relational reality. The issue, transgression, or pain may be moving outward and loosening its grip on the individual and family, but the movement is gradual. Recurring memories of the past are like waves that continue to wash up over the family even as their strength and intensity diminish.

There have been instances in work with people on forgiveness in which change was immediate, clear, and apparently totally secure from the ravages of the past. But usually in forgiveness therapy healing and building intergenerational family strength occur as a slow process. Often, the therapist and the individual must be willing to go over the same past issues many times as the effects and nuances of the damage play out in different ways. Progress, growth, and healing are very much at a "two steps forward, one step back" pace. Also, it is important for the therapist to coach the individual and the family as to the likelihood that the work of forgiveness may not be resolved completely even after therapy is over. Like most therapy, the reality of the relational work will play out for the years to come as the family members understand themselves and their interactions more and learn how to self-correct in efforts to give to one another.

## ASSESSMENT AND FORGIVENESS

The great passenger liner *Titanic* will always occupy a place of special interest and fascination. She was the epitome of prestige and strength, and there was no finer ship ever built. When she sailed from Southampton on her maiden voyage in April of 1912 and struck an iceberg and sank with the loss of over 1500 lives, the mystery and mystique of the *Titanic* seemed to be sealed in the icy depth of the Atlantic. But even as the *Titanic* lay at a depth of over 1300 feet, the public wondered for 75 years at the her fate and what secrets lay below. Hollywood even created a movie entitled *Raise the Titanic,* giving voice to our longing to see the great ship again.

Our dreams were realized when Robert Ballard found the *Titanic* in 1985. With a motorized sled containing cameras called the *Argo*, he showed all of us the reality concerning the fate of the great ship. True, it had an awesome and silent splendor to it as the ship's shape was shadowed on the ocean floor. But the camera on the *Argo* also revealed a tortured and painful end to the massive structure. The ship was ripped open by the iceberg like a can opener across many of its watertight compartments. The cruel pressure forces at such a tremendous depth literally tore the *Titanic* in two. Our fascination and Hollywood dreams ran smack into reality—the *Titanic* would never be raised, and salvage of anything from the ship was improbable.

In dealing with families where there has been a severe violation of love and trust, the therapist must realize the harsh reality of the damage. People's lives are not painful and in turmoil because they simply refuse to go on and "leave the past behind." They are not necessarily weak because they are unable to "pull themselves up by their bootstraps." People are asking the therapist for help because the violation of love and trust has sunk the family ship and it lies in a terrible mess hidden from most of the world. When forgiveness is helpful to families, it is the therapist's job to help the family members assess the damage accurately and provide consultation and assistance on how best to handle the damage.

### Salvage or Restoration?

In order to be helpful to the family, the therapist must clearly have in mind the distinct difference between salvage and restoration efforts. Salvage efforts help the individual understand how the family relationships came to be in a wreck. They seek to clarify the damaged parts of the family and sort them from the possible strengths. Then finally, salvage efforts help the individual integrate the reality of the damaged past so it can be avoided in future relationships and utilize the intergenerational strengths to address the emotional pain the family caused. But this salvage effort occurs under the knowledge and reality that the family relationships are probably too far gone to be raised to a seaworthy condition.

Restoration is a very different proposition in therapy. Restoration efforts are aimed at actually raising the "family ship" and repairing it to acceptable working condition. Restoration demands that the family members who sunk the ship all cooperate to understand the damage and learn how to avoid the violations in the future. It is harder work, but offers hope to the individual and the family that mistakes can be corrected and new family legacies can be written.

In therapy, salvage efforts are the work of the first two stations of exonerating, while restoration efforts are that of the second two stations of forgiving. Assessing the appropriateness of exonerating or forgiving is difficult because the choice is not based on the severity of the violation. In my experience, there is no incest, abuse, or manipulation so severe that it automatically removes the possibility of forgiving. At the same time, less violent and overt acts are no guarantee that forgiving will be easier to accomplish. As people are more movable, changeable, and responsible with regard to their positions with family members, the more potential there is in the work of forgiveness. It is this potential for difference that is the most important factor in determining salvage or restoration efforts. Unjust violation was the root of the breakdown of trust and justice. As the potential for difference increases, the potential for restoration of love and trust increases.

While restoration of family relationships is probably preferable in terms of long-term intergenerational love and trust, it is not always feasible because the family or individual is too threatened or too destructive. For a therapist to try to force the second two stations of forgiving on a family is like forcing them to rearrange the furnishings on a sinking ship. The family will work hard and still attain a sad and regrettable result. On the other hand, it is just as inappropriate for a therapist to hold an individual or family back from the work of restoration just because it is risky business. Many times, the riskier the family relationships, the greater the payoff in terms of love and trust resources.

Accurate assessment of the appropriateness of exonerating or forgiving is difficult at best. The therapist must rely heavily upon the reports of the individual and family and the "feel" of their relationships with one another. In proceeding with the work of forgiveness, a therapist is not a judge of reality, predictor of the future, or interpreter of the past. The therapist is simply an assistant to the individual or family as a caddie is to a golfer. It is the job of the therapist to help the individual read the conditions and lay of the course and then make suggestions based on the therapist's previous experience that might be useful in playing the course. But the shots and the decisions are clearly left to the individuals and families for they are the ones who will succeed or fail and deal with the responsibility for their actions.

The individual or family knows the family history and lineage much better than any therapist ever will and is often a better judge of the strengths and weaknesses that exist in the family. But while the therapist cannot be responsible alone for making the decisions concerning exonerating and forgiving, the therapist must certainly have a clear picture of what he or she is trying to help the individual or family accomplish.

Many times a therapist will start out to help a family member in the work of forgiveness by exonerating through insight and understanding and later find out that there is real potential for forgiving in the second two stations. Likewise, often the therapist works in a well-meaning way toward restoration and forgiving only to discover that the best that can be accomplished at the time is exoneration. Insight and understanding most often enhance the work of forgiving in the last two stations. For this reason, I have most often found them a safe place to begin the therapeutic work of forgiveness with clients. But for the therapist to know when work is too risky or not appropriate, he or she must keep a close watch on the relational reality of the family. The individual and family will shift in their potential and desire for forgiveness, and the therapist must rely heavily on intuition in directing the family.

## THE ROLE OF THE THERAPIST

Each therapist has a different therapeutic style. Many are primarily empathizers and supporters, while others are more like directors and coaches. But most therapists understand the need for variation and will utilize different styles in order to help clients. The work of forgiveness includes different techniques in the work of exonerating and in that of forgiving, and also in the two stations of each. Using different emphases and techniques in each station, a therapist will serve in a number of therapeutic roles with the individual and family as forgiveness is accomplished.

### The Role in Insight

The station of insight is essential if the individual in the family is going to be able to recognize the mechanisms by which family pain and injustice are perpetuated. Therapists can usually see these patterns and transactions quite objectively because they are outside of the emotional field of the family. But to individuals who are tied to the emotional bonds of the family and have been damaged, objectivity is very difficult. They have trusted and depended upon the family for love and have been violated in some manner. They are likely to feel all the desire and need for the love and trust deserved and simultaneously feel the frustration and resentment for the violations they have endured. This mix of emotion often leads an individual to an inability to clearly delineate the patterns and hierarchy by which the pain and damage are perpetuated and even the specifics of why interactions are so painful.

When the individual or family is seeking to do the work of forgiveness in the station of insight, it is important for the therapist to be able to highlight in an objective manner the methods by which love and trust are violated. This objectivity helps clarify the pain to the individual and assists him or her in the effort to separate the emotional turmoil from the transactions that occur in the family. After these transactions and patterns are clarified, then the therapist can assist the individual with strategies to protect him or her from the emotional ravages the family might perpetuate and even challenge the family system in such a way that it can never be the same.

The therapist, therefore, helping an individual or family in the station of insight must consistently ask penetrating questions to clearly understand the complete cycle of interactions that cause pain or damage. This delineation can take place in several ways using several possible techniques. Boscolo, Cecchin, Hoffman, and Penn (1987) describe how patterns in the family are demonstrated in communication, both verbal and nonverbal. The original Milan group used circular questions to clarify confused family patterns in families with problems and introduced new feedback to the family. The therapist helping an individual or family work through forgiveness can utilize circular questioning in much the same way to reveal harmful patterns and suggest new strategies for dealing with pain.

In a similar vein, tracking (Minuchin, 1974) can be used by the therapist to detail specific patterns of behavior and feelings in the family. The basic technique of tracking is for the therapist to set up transactions and process using the language of the individual and family to identify the structure and elements that contribute to the harmful or dysfunctional patterns.

Many times it is helpful for the therapist, individual, and family to watch the method the family used or uses to perpetuate injustice by having the individual or family act out a hurtful interaction using a role play or sculpting. In role play members of the family take on the different perspectives of others in the family or even engage in role reversal. In sculpting (Satir, 1967; Papp, Silverstein,

& Carter, 1973), the individual or family symbolizes emotional process or realities in the family by spatial position, posture, or representative actions or feelings. Role play and sculpting are particularly helpful because they usually reveal an emotional dimension of the damaging family transaction that may not become available in normal questioning and tracking.

No matter the technique used, therapists should seek to use their objectivity to clarify to the individual and family two processes. First, the objectivity is needed to make clear to the individual or family the personal identification and feelings of each member. In this manner, members are better able to relate their feelings about unjustified harm in the family and identify the root of their pain. Second, the objectivity should clearly dramatize the roles in the family and the interactional process that connects the family system that violated love and trust. This clarification allows the therapist, individual, and family to propose changes in the roles or interactions that at the least should protect the members from future violations of love and trust.

### The Role in Understanding

The station of understanding is important in the work of forgiveness in its ability to assist damaged persons in making identification with the circumstances, situations, and people associated with the relational injustice. This identification, therefore, provides a mechanism to alleviate some of the pain and trauma associated with undeserved hurt. Part of the objectivity a therapist should maintain in any case is the ability to empathize with and understand the relational actions of all family members. As stated before, while individuals are clearly responsible for their actions in relationships, they each come from a past of family and circumstantial experiences that may twist their motives into destructive and self-justifying actions. In many ways, family members who harm others are victims of past and present injustices themselves. While not excusing such destructive actions, the therapist is in a position to shed light on the victimizer that makes it possible for the victim to understand the relational harm in a different way. This understanding then opens the possibility for both the victim and the victimizer to remove the burden of blame and culpability for past actions and, in many cases, sets the stage for possible trustworthy relating.

The primary technique used by the therapist in making and maintaining identification with all relational parties in the family is called *multidirected partiality*. Boszormenyi-Nagy and Krasner (1986) describe multidirected partiality as the therapist's effort to surface each family member's interest and viewpoint in the relational ledger in the family. After these interests and view-points are surfaced, the therapist then supports the different "sides" of each family member. This fulfills entitlement require-ments of each member of the family and lends recognition and justification to each particular interest. It is important to note that multidirected partiality is not neutrality. Neutrality refuses to acknowledge any side as being right or wrong. Multidirected partiality fully supports the interests and perspectives of an individual family member. However, the therapist's partiality does not extend to excusing destructive actions of any person or nullifying another family member's interest or perspective. Multidirected partiality simply gives credence and proper hearing in turn to each person and perspective involved in the relational damage.

The technique of multidirected partiality is so powerful in the work of forgiveness because as family members are recognized for their own perspectives and responsibilities in the damaged relationships, they are more willing to credit and recognize others' perspectives and responsibilities. In a very elemental manner, this crediting is the initial step in rebuilding trust to relationships. It is essential that the therapist be partial to all relational parties involved in the damaged family even if all the family members are not present. The therapist is not just the advocate and supporter of one person who has been unjustly damaged, but the advocate and supporter of all the family "victims." Multidirected partiality involves the therapist's empathizing with each family member, crediting his or her relational concerns, then expecting responsible relational action in the future (Boszormenyi-Nagy & Krasner, 1986). As the therapist makes this identification with relational victims and culprits alike, the victims of unjust family actions are better able to make identification with and understand the family members who perpetrated the pain.

Another helpful technique that the therapist may utilize in order to assist the individual or family with understanding is the construction of a family genogram (McGoldrick & Gerson, 1985). Genograms are helpful in assisting a victim of relational damage in the effort to understand how life cycle occurrences, past events, and patterns have affected the family and how these events and patterns may have been transmitted for generations. The genogram also often reveals how a victim's current behavior may relate to the intergenerational transmission of the family, thereby expanding the understanding and possible empathy the victim will have for other family members.

Individuals who have suffered unjust trauma in their families often carry damage from their childhoods. Since children often understand their families in very simplistic or distorted ways, relational damage may result in the victim's internalizing a deep emotional pain from only one perspective or for only one possible reason. These limited perspectives and this deep emotional pain are often left intact until adulthood. Imagery is sometimes useful to recapitulate the events that were damaging to assist the victim in considering and identifying different perspectives, reasons, and possible myths associated with the trauma. As subjective impressions of the relational trauma are reconsidered, the victim's understanding of the unjust action is broadened and identification with the victimizer is possible. Morrison (1981) makes several suggestions in utilizing guided imagery not only to deal with painful trauma with new considerations but also to recall times when the family was loving and trustworthy to produce a balanced perspective of the victim's past.

## The Role in Giving the Opportunity for Compensation

In many ways, the two stations in forgiving offer more caveats to therapy. First, there is real relational risk to the victims as they expose themselves to the possibility of more unloving or untrustworthy relationships. Second, more relational parties are involved in the therapy in an overt manner, thereby increasing the likelihood that some member will be vindictive, defensive, or damaging. Finally, the rudiments of trust building in a damaged family are usually met with extreme caution and suspicion by family members, and so energy and momentum toward love and trust are slow to develop. The therapist who works with an individual and family in these two stations in the work of forgiveness must be extremely aware of these caveats and realistic as to their effects in the therapeutic effort.

Giving the opportunity for compensation allows the victim to address past relational trauma by experiencing trustworthy and loving transactions with the person who caused the original pain. Since this opportunity for compensation does not directly address the original trauma, it is important that the therapist help victims carefully assess their feelings toward the future relationship and develop realistic expectations of what the relationship should be in the future.

The first effort of the therapist in helping the victim develop this new relational perspective is to work with the victim in acceptance of the damage and status of the current relationship. This essentially is ensuring that the intense mourning and anger that may immobilize the therapeutic effort have oscillated enough for the victim to be able to see the victimizer without experiencing intense emotional reactions such as depression or rage. Next, the therapist should assist the victim in developing a plan of interaction that will give the victimizer the opportunity to demonstrate love and trust in a sequential manner. Most often, victims want victimizers to demonstrate love and trust in a "too much, too fast" fashion. One way to help victims maintain their willingness to accept small efforts in rebuilding love and trust is for the therapist to role-play interactions with the victim with the victim taking the role of the victimizer. This broadens the victim's perspective and assists in the recognition of effort on the victimizer's part. It is important, as real interactions between the victim and victimizer occur, for the therapist to help the victim be willing to see small efforts on the part of the victimizer as worthy and to give them appropriate credit.

The third concentration of effort of the therapist assisting in this station should be to keep the expected outcomes of the relationship between the victim and victimizer realistic. As mentioned before, mistakes will be made by both relational parties that will not build love and trust. The therapist must convey to the victim that these mistakes will not make a future relationship impossible and do not necessarily mean that the victimizer is reverting to past irresponsibility. It is often useful for the therapist to help the victim develop a written ledger or contract that clearly specifies his or her expectations and obligations in the current interaction with the victimizer. This gives both the victim and the therapist a clear guide to the performance expectations. The therapist can then assist the victim in developing and modifying the contract so that it both is realistic and allows for minor infractions. This same contract can then be used in crediting the victimizer with appropriate love and trust when interactions are successful.

Many times, victims will want old issues addressed that were unjust and caused pain, but are unwilling to overtly bring up the issue with the relational culprit. It is sometimes possible to make some interactions between the victim and victimizer that are symbolic representations. For instance, a victim may plan a trip to a past residence where a victimizer inflicted pain or trauma. Once at the residence, the victim and victimizer may have a simple conversation about a particular place or time that does not involve the relational trauma. The therapist can help the victim make this very simple interaction a symbol for the possibility and reality of the changed relationship. Other interactions may center around the technique of symbolic gift giving as discussed by Sherman and Fredman (1986). These symbolic gifts and interactions can have a powerful effect in addressing old and unjustified trauma in an indirect manner.

## The Role in the Overt Act of Forgiving

The fourth station in the work of forgiveness involves at least two people coming together to address the past damage and hurt in a direct and overt manner. The possibility of such an effort turning into a destructive, defensive, and blaming session is high. But with such risks, there is also tremendous potential for relational rebirthing. It is the role of the therapist to ensure in this fourth station that the effort to forgive remains constructive and does not become destructive.

In relational reconstruction in the overt act of forgiving, it is usually most helpful for the therapist to take on the role of relational mediator or coach. For the work of forgiving to be accomplished in this station, the victim and victimizer must come to agreement on the violation, acknowledgment of responsibility, apology, and promise for a future relationship. This usually entails tough face-to-face bargaining and communication between the victim and victimizer. The therapist can greatly assist the individuals in this effort in clarifying communication and keeping the effort on track to a productive end. In maintaining this productive and constructive effort, the therapist will often have to be a very directive "coach." This may involve cutting off destructive comments or guiding the relational parties in demonstrations of what each might say.

Rituals are often extremely helpful in the effort to accomplish the overt act of forgiving. Many times, both the victim and the victimizer develop specific defensive and symptomatic interactions in order to deal with the pain and trauma associated with the past. These interactions only serve to perpetuate the past pain and serve as a real interactional obstacle to forgiving. As described by Palazzoli, Boscolo, Cecchin, and Prata (1978), a prescribed ritual with corresponding new interactions can serve as a substitution for the old dysfunctional pattern. These rituals can then serve as a touchstone to both the victim and the victimizer in remembering new patterns and rejecting old and inappropriate behaviors associated with past trauma. Rituals can also serve as powerful symbols (Imber-Black, 1988a) that give meaning to the forgiving process and thereby enhance the power of the overt act to affect future interactions and relations. In order to construct and utilize rituals effectively in this station, the therapist must clearly understand the system and the intergenerational and cultural influences on the distressed family.

## FAMILY OF ORIGIN ISSUES AND THE THERAPIST

Whitaker (1982) warned of the dangers of *countertransference*, or the reexperiencing of feelings on the therapist's part in response to a clinical family. A therapist who does not guard against such countertransference is likely to have distorted feelings toward individuals or families to the extent that it clouds good clinical judgment. For instance, a therapist who was sexually abused and is still enraged by the violation may believe that an individual who suffered sexual abuse should never forgive or have any relationship at all with the perpetrator. In the same vein, an abused therapist who has forgiven his or her abuser successfully may expect nothing less of a similarly abused individual in therapy.

The relational reality of any family is complex enough without therapists injecting their own relational issues. In the work of forgiveness, countertransference can be especially damaging as therapists may be tempted to be too empathetic with a victim, too harsh or distant to a victimizer, or too manipulative in the forgiving process. Bad therapeutic judgment in the work of forgiveness can have damaging intergenerational results; therefore, therapists must keep their family of origin experiences in the forefront of their minds so as to not mix their own experiences with the pasts of their clients.

Good intergenerational therapists are those who not only know their issues in their family of origin, but also are willing to deal with them in a responsible and trustworthy manner. If therapists are unwilling to deal with their past in an overt manner, then it makes sense that their past family issues will seep covertly into their work with a clinical family.

*Chapter Seven*

# CLINICAL APPLICATION OF INSIGHT

A few years ago I had the pleasure of viewing a portrait of Georges Clemenceau painted by Monet at the Kimbell Art Museum in Fort Worth, Texas. I have always been fascinated with the Impressionists. From a closer perspective, the portrait was nothing more than dabs and blotches of color. But with just one or two steps back, the striking features of the fiery French leader emerged. Perspective with Impressionistic work truly makes all the difference in the world. Such is the truth with helping an individual or family negotiate the work of forgiveness in the station of insight. Family situations that appear to be unmitigated messes and hopelessly confusing might take on clearer features as the perspective on the family and relationships is shifted. This is the work of therapy in the station of insight: to shift the perspective of the individual and family to gain insight on how damage was perpetrated and is perpetuated so further damage can be prevented.

Such insight is essential in the work of forgiveness if trustworthy relationships are to ever be established in the intergenerational group. If individuals cannot see how the relational injustice occurred in the family and what influences perpetuated the pain, they will be subjugated to confusion and likely suffer the turmoil of pain, and perhaps even recycle the untrustworthy action through destructive entitlement. If individuals are to get on the road of forgiveness, they must be reasonably assured that there is knowledge and behavior that can be implemented to protect themselves and loved ones from future injustice. The purpose of this chapter is to demonstrate how this work of insight proceeds in therapy.

## CASE EXAMPLE: "I'M ABOUT TO GO CRAZY"

Of course, intergenerational family relationships are quite complex in every way. In station one of forgiveness, insight into the complexity of the intergenerational framework and how injustice occurs in the family is achieved in therapy in a gradual manner. As therapy proceeds, small insights spaced further apart in time sometimes allow an individual or family to build more sweeping connections of insight at a quicker pace. In a very real sense, insight builds and leads to further insight. Therefore, therapy usually entails the therapist's helping the individual or family gain initial small insights and then guiding them in how to achieve their own clearer perspectives on the intergenerational damage in order to prevent further or future pain.

In the following case example, a middle-aged divorced woman and mother of four children was experiencing various ailments, including high blood pressure, aching in the joints, spastic colon, and insomnia. After a complete medical exam yielded no physical causes for the problems, the woman was referred to therapy. She had a very low education level and had married relatively young. She and her former husband had had a tumultuous marriage that lasted 22 years and finally ended in divorce eight years earlier. Although she worked very hard, her lack of education locked her into low-paying jobs. Her children, who ranged in age from 21 to nine, all currently lived with her in a small two-bedroom apartment. Obviously, the day-to-day stress level of the woman was very high. However, she reported that her life had always been stressful and in fact had been very much worse at other times. The woman said that she had always worked very hard and saw stress as "just part of life." However, she said that her current distress was caused by tremendous emotional pain she could not identify. Her confusion over her situation was extremely evident in the first session.

THERAPIST: It seems very difficult for you to name the pain that you feel.

WOMAN: I'm so confused. I've worked all my life and been able to make it. I've been thrown out on the streets and had to survive with nothing. But now it's like I just can't go on anymore. I wake up at night and am in a cold sweat. I'm afraid to go back to sleep. Sometimes I am so tied up inside that just the slightest thing can set me off. Sometimes I feel like I'm going to explode! Then I'll feel so alone and depressed. I will cry for hours at a time. I've wondered if I'm going through the change.

THERAPIST: Did your physical indicate that you might be going through menopause?

WOMAN: No. I asked my doctor about it specifically. I wish I could blame this on menopause, but I know down deep that there is something bad inside. *(starts to cry)* I'm so afraid of what is on the inside, but I can't remember anything. I know it's tying me up in knots but I don't know if I can handle it. Sometimes I think I'm about to go crazy!

When there is some type of unjustified trauma in the intergenerational past, memory blocks and cutoffs are not unusual. The pain the woman felt, however, appeared to be connected to something she was unable to put into words. Since the woman was faced with a myriad of potential stressors, any one of which could produce painful emotional turmoil or depression, the therapist moved cautiously in trying to help her connect the pain she felt with the past so as to not appear insensitive to her current situation. Although the woman continued to acknowledge the stress, she remained convinced that her pain was "deep inside."

The therapist decided to join with the woman's assessment and try to help her identify some of the possible issues that were causing the pain. Throughout the therapy, however, the therapist continued to remain sensitive to the current family issues and stress by complimenting the woman on her resourceful ability to survive and nurture her children through tumultuous circumstances.

THERAPIST: If you feel the pain is coming from the inside, it might be something in your past. What do you think?

WOMAN: I know it is in the past, but I can't remember. I'm not sure that I want to remember what happened. I think there may be something bad.

THERAPIST: I don't know you that well. But from what you have already told me, I know that you're a woman of incredible strength to be able to come from an unhappy marriage and make a way for yourself and your children. I believe that when people are as strong as you have demonstrated, they are basically good. My hunches tell me that your strength and goodness would outweigh any bad that is on the inside.

WOMAN: All I've done is survive. I know what it feels like to be scared though.

THERAPIST: I would imagine so. That speaks even more for your strength. You have been able to survive even when you were scared. Even though you are scared now, I believe that you will survive.

WOMAN: (*much calmer*) Where should I begin? I don't know where to start.

THERAPIST: Why don't we start with just a little piece of your pain. We will be working together for quite a while, so we don't want to try to deal with everything all at once. Let's just take a little of what you do remember about your past.

Many times when individuals with damaged family pasts have blocked the trauma through memory lapses, the pain of facing past issues may seem overwhelming. It is essential for the therapist to use clients' strengths to enable them to face the past that is buried alive in their psyche. As clients gain strength, they gain more confidence in the process of looking back and inward to their pain. Therefore, it is not unusual for clients to remember more and more of the past as they believe that the past can be dealt with successfully.

In this case and in many others, the woman's present turmoil indicated that the pain she felt was not connected to just one traumatic injustice in the family past. Rather, the injustice in the woman's family was multifaceted, with numerous and repeated instances of relational damage. As the woman began to identify some of her family background, the multidimensional turmoil began to become clearer. She stated that she was the oldest of five daughters in her family and that her mother married at 15. The marriage was evidently extremely unstable as the woman remembered lengthy separations when she was a girl. She said that she was always fearful of her father and was not sure that he ever loved her or any of her sisters. Although she stated that she believed that her mother loved her, her descriptions of her mother indicated that the mother was very fragile. She also had very vague recollections of herself and her sisters being shifted around to several caretakers. When the woman spoke of one set of caretakers in particular, she became extremely tense.

The emotional field in the intergenerational family is often left intact from one generation to the next. Many times, the therapist can access information that is locked away in the past by accessing the emotional field in the present. In the next session, the therapist started trying to help the woman specify the pain.

THERAPIST: When was the last time you saw your mother?

WOMAN: Last summer. I went to a family reunion.

THERAPIST: Tell me what it is like to be around your mother.

WOMAN: It's funny. When I was out there, I wanted to stay real bad. I would joke around and say that I was going to move in with her. But it's like my mother doesn't really want me there. I mean she loves me, but she don't want me too close. She's remarried and has her own life now.

THERAPIST: She has a new life?

WOMAN: Yeah.

THERAPIST: A new life. It sounds like the new life doesn't leave much room for people like you. People from the past.

WOMAN: The past was really bad for all of us. There are things that I want to ask my mother about but I'm afraid that it would make her too upset. I want to ask her...*[long pause]* I want to ask her about some things I remembered.

THERAPIST: Tell me about what you remembered.

WOMAN: *(long pause)* My mom was too young when she married. When she'd fight with my dad, he would just leave for a long time. I don't think she could handle us kids. I really don't remember where she went.

THERAPIST: Did she leave you?

WOMAN: No, I don't think so. It was like she would take me places and leave me. I remember having terrible fights with her. *(starts to cry)* I wanted her to be around but she couldn't handle me. I

was on my own and I didn't know anything. I got
involved with a boy and I got pregnant. My
mom took me to this place like an unwed
mothers' place, but it was like a reformatory. No
one could ever come and see me. *(pause)* ...or
no one ever did. I thought I was going to have to
stay there the rest of my life because I got pregnant. After my baby was born, they took it
away. I guess someone adopted it. I don't even
know if it was a boy or a girl.

THERAPIST: Were you able to go back home ever?

WOMAN: Yeah. She came and got me, but we had the
same trouble. I think two years later I fell in love
with a neighbor boy and got pregnant again.
*(sternly)* This time she sent me away to a bad
place. It was out of town. I think he [the boy]
was sent someplace too, and we never got to see
each other again. I never saw him again! She
sent me to this place where there were only nuns.
I wasn't allowed to talk or see nobody. They
didn't let me see my baby when it was born.
They just gave it away again. I was never
allowed to see him [the boy] again, and I really
loved him.

Here the woman started accessing some of the specifics about
her past that caused her pain and, at the same time, anger
concerning the injustice. When the woman talked about how her
mother had separated herself from the past, she recalled a previous
experience when her mother separated from her. The woman
indicated that her mother was only 15 when she had her and
evidently became overwhelmed easily with the care of five
children. When the woman became pregnant the first time
(probably around age 13), she was put in someone else's care.
Feeling already that she was responsible for her own care, she now
was abandoned by her mother. The anger over the second

pregnancy indicated that the woman may have wanted more control and saw her mother's effort to send her to a convent as clearly wrong.

The picture was now beginning to develop of a young mother who was overwhelmed by a bad marriage and was unable to care for her children. The early pregnancies left the therapist to wonder if there had been sexual abuse in the woman's childhood or if the first pregnancy was a result of a rape. In the next session, the therapist again taps into the woman's past by accessing the present emotional field.

THERAPIST: It sounds to me that you had to learn to take care of yourself from a very early age. Your mother seemed to not be able to take care of herself and her children. You married very young too and have had a difficult marriage. But you have been able to hang in there.

WOMAN: I worry about what I have done. Sometimes I just can't take it and I go back to the bedroom and cry for hours. *(begins to cry)* I worry especially about my daughter. I know I lean on her too much. She takes care of me and I know that's wrong.

THERAPIST: You know it's wrong. How do you know?

WOMAN: I know because I know what it feels like. I know how scared I got when my mom was too sad. I felt like I had to take care of her because if I didn't, she would go crazy. I was always scared she would lose it.

THERAPIST: Is that what it still feels like with your mom?

WOMAN: *(crying harder with long pauses)* Yes. It was so bad. I didn't know how to take care of my mom. If she just would have pulled herself together, I think I would have been okay. She would get depressed and just ship us kids off to different homes. I think she knew that was the wrong thing

THERPIST: She shipped all of you off? Where?

WOMAN: To a neighbor's. Sometimes she would keep my youngest sister, but I was made to live at these people's house a lot.

THERAPIST: Things were difficult. How about your father? Did you ever stay with him?

WOMAN: My dad drank so much. He and my mom used to fight and they would beat each other up. *(laughing while still tearful)* I'm not sure who got the worst of it! *(pause, then more serious)* I can remember my father coming to see us a few times, but he never took us. He remarried. He would always say things to us kids about mom. *(long pause)* I remember one time he had us in the car and said he was going to drive us over the cliff.

THERAPIST: Do you think he was serious?

WOMAN: I don't know. He was so unhappy. After he remarried he had two more kids and I've only talked to him twice since then. I really don't even know where he lives for sure. It's like he didn't want to ever remember my mom and we reminded him of her.

The woman had clearly been in a very destructive situation growing up. Not only was she required to be the emotional and sometimes physical caretaker for her mother, there were times where the mother would apparently abandon her. Her father, unable to deal responsibly with his former marriage and children, made damaging threats and then abandoned the children entirely. It is easy to understand why the woman struggled so for survival and was in severe emotional pain. Very simply, the woman grew up in such an unstable environment that the only person she really felt cared for her was her young daughter. Therefore, even though she knew it is wrong to parentify her own daughter, the intergenerational damage was still transmitted. The therapist, however, was careful to point out to the woman that even though she leaned on her daughter inappropriately at times, she had never abandoned her daughter. The woman pledged to no longer use her daughter for emotional comfort and was clearly strengthened by the perspective that she had always remained with her children.

Although the therapy was painful through the first four sessions, the therapist and the woman had clearly begun to identify where the painful lack of love and trust had originated. In addition to the situation with her mother and father, she stated that she also felt that her siblings did not want her around and felt uneasy with her. Also, the woman told of the sad saga of her struggle to stay married to an alcoholic and physically abusive husband. The woman still had large gaps in her memory, but as she was helped to identify the specific incidents of injustice in her family, her confidence was built and her physical problems began to decrease. At the beginning of the sixth session, the woman reported that she had remembered being sexually abused.

WOMAN:      I need to tell you something that I remembered
            this week. I woke up one night cold and sweat-
            ing. I could feel it just like it had happened.
            *(pause)* I don't know if I can get it out.
THERAPIST:  Don't rush yourself. If you are not ready to tell
            me, I can certainly wait until you are.
WOMAN:      Remember I told you that my mother used to
            leave me with some neighbors. I have always
            hated that man. I used to tell my mother that and
            she used to tell me that they were so good to me.
            Well, I remember why I hate him. *(long pause)*
            He used to come into the room where I slept and
            touch me all over. *(starts to cry)* I'm so
            ashamed.
THERAPIST:  It's okay. You were young and he was old.
WOMAN:      This is the worst... *(pause)* ...there was another.
            There was boy who used to stay with them too.

This man would make me and this boy do things
in front of him. *(starts to sob)* I just didn't know
what to do! This happened a lot! I hated that
couple.

THERAPIST: *(after a long pause, he reaches out and takes her hand)* It's okay. There was nobody there to
protect you. You were alone. But you are not
alone now.

WOMAN: I've figured out that my mom knew something
was wrong. She had to know something was
wrong by the way I hated them. But she kept on
sending me there and leaving me. I think she
must have known.

It is difficult to know exactly what triggered the intense
emotional pain that brought the woman to therapy. Perhaps it was
a life cycle memory when her own daughter reached the age when
she was sexually abused. Maybe the intense situational stress of
the woman isolated her to the point of feeling alone and abandoned. At any rate, the woman was now clearly identifying the
violations in the relational ethics dimension that caused her pain
and, in her mind, the most severe violation of all: being abandoned
by her irresponsible parents and left to be repeatedly sexually
abused. Recognition of the damage now opened new possibilities
to the woman to change the family system in such a way that she
would never again become a victim. In essence, the woman had
started the difficult work of forgiveness in her family by gaining
initial insight into her past.

The therapist worked with the woman for the next two sessions
in identifying several behaviors and feelings associated with the
relational trauma she had experienced. In identifying these
feelings, the woman was very responsive to applying herself to
learning how she could prevent passing along some of the
emotional trauma she experienced to her children, and especially
her daughter. This was a clearer indication that she was gaining
further insight into her damaged past. This protection of her own

family, combined with knowing that she could handle the memories of her past without "going crazy," enabled the woman to consider how she could address these old family wounds.

As mentioned before in Chapter Two, the system and organization in the family that originally allowed the damaging transactions to violate individuals will continue to feel just as dangerous and threatening to the victim if it is unchecked. From all appearances and descriptions, the emotional field and transactions in this woman's family had not shifted significantly since she was a child. Therefore, the woman continued to feel victimized by the family because she felt they did not love her and they were untrustworthy.

Part of the difficult work of insight is helping the victim realize that there are different actions, patterns, and kinds of communication that will effectively change the family system and ensure that the victim will be protected from future emotional damage. The ability to prevent *and feel protected from* damage the family system can perpetuate is an essential step in forgiveness. If one still feels victimized by a family system, he or she will be unable to make any movement toward trustworthy relationships.

As a young girl, the woman was a victim of an abusive, immature, and uneducated household. She came to the insight that when she was a girl she had had very few options in preventing the damage because so many of the adults around her were conspirators (knowingly and unknowingly) in the abuse. She had internalized this untrustworthy and unloving atmosphere into an insecure and unworthy self-image. Even though the woman was now decades older, she still carried the insecure and unworthy self-image and reacted in the family system much the same way she did when she was a girl. In the eighth session, the therapist now began the work of helping the woman gain insight into the family transactions that would help her gain better control and protect herself from the unfair and damaging relationships. Again, in order to access the emotional field of the past, the therapist began with the woman's present family relationships.

THERAPIST: Your background has caused you a lot of pain. Do you ever worry about your children and pain that they may experience as adults?

WOMAN: I think about that a lot. I know that they will have some hard things to deal with, but I'm just going to keep trying to do better. Like you said, I haven't done everything right but I'm sure going to make sure they know that I love them. I have thought about my daughter a lot. I've wondered if she ever was abused. I've tried to make sure that nothing would ever happen to her. I don't think it has. I don't think [my former husband] ever did anything to her.

THERAPIST: If she ever had been abused or if anything awful had ever happened to her, what would you want her to do?

WOMAN: I would want her to know that she didn't have to put up with that. I would want her to tell me, and I'd make sure that whoever did that to her went to jail!

THERAPIST: You would want her to tell you, and then you would protect her. I know that's true. I've seen how you are becoming more and more sure of yourself. But when you were sexually abused, you were scared to tell anyone.

WOMAN: That's true. I didn't think my mom would believe me. I'm really not sure she could handle it. *(pause)* I don't think she'd want to hear it. She wouldn't believe it.

THERAPIST: Is there a chance that if something awful happened to your daughter like it happened to you, that she would be scared to tell you?

WOMAN: *(long pause)* I've never looked at it that way. She really does feel like she needs to take care of me sometimes. Even though we baby her, I know she worries about me.

THERAPIST: It is a real gift you give to your daughter when you reassure her that she can tell you anything. How could you go about making sure that your daughter wouldn't be scared?

WOMAN: I could tell her that I want her to tell me anything like that. That's the biggest thing. You know, I really knew that my mom didn't want to hear that something bad had happened to me. I wouldn't want that for my girl. I guess I could tell her that I wanted her to tell me and then tell her that I can hear anything. I wouldn't want her to be alone like I was.

Here we see that the woman was making substantial progress in gaining insight. She clearly believed that the most essential thing in protecting her daughter was ensuring that the daughter knew that she wanted to know and that she was able to handle the knowledge appropriately. These were the essential elements that were lacking in her relationship with her own mother when she was a girl. With this emotional field clearly accessed, the therapist could move the woman to appropriate action not only with her daughter but also with her mother.

THERAPIST: You said that your daughter takes care of you sometimes. Do you think you could handle it if your daughter told you that she had been abused some way?

WOMAN: (*very slowly*) I know it would just tear me apart. I worry about some of the things that have happened to her. I know that she wasn't sexually abused, but I know that she's seen and heard things she shouldn't have. *[pause]* But I would want to know. I wouldn't want her to be alone. I'd want to know so I could help her and make sure it didn't happen again.

THERAPIST: I wonder if there is a chance that your mother felt

| | |
|---|---|
| | like you. You picked up that your mother didn't want to know how you were abused, but deep down, there was part of her that wanted to protect you. |
| WOMAN: | I don't know. Maybe. |
| THERAPIST: | Well, even if she didn't want to know, it was her responsibility as a parent to protect you. |
| WOMAN: | That's true. I may not want to hear something, but I've got to make sure that my daughter is safe. Not hearing it isn't going to make it go away. |
| THERAPIST: | I agree. Not talking about what happened to you all those years certainly did not make it go away. It's still here. If something awful happened to your daughter, you would want to know and you would want to protect her. When you were sexually abused, you believed no one wanted to know and there was no one to protect you. You are a woman now. Maybe you could want people to know and protect yourself. |
| WOMAN: | I've thought about telling somebody, but I don't know. I guess I'm still afraid that they will not believe me. My mom is always saying the past is the past. Leave it lie. |
| THERAPIST: | There is some wisdom in that statement. But even though the past is buried in your family, it is buried alive. It will not let you rest until some of it is acknowledged. Besides, I'm concerned that if you can't learn to protect yourself in your family now, you won't know exactly how to protect your daughter. |
| WOMAN: | How can they hurt me? I'm so far away. |
| THERAPIST: | They may be far away in distance, but they are the same people that hurt you long ago. As long as they don't change, you still hurt inside because you know that they could hurt you again. |

WOMAN:      You're right.  When I saw them last year at the
            reunion I was hurt by the way they treated me.  I
            don't know how I could talk to them.  I have
            never told anyone about these things except you.
THERAPIST:  Well you don't have to talk about all the abuse all
            at once.  Maybe if you just took a little bit of the
            abuse you went through and communicated it to
            part of the family.  Just enough to let them know
            that you weren't going to keep the secret any
            longer.  Just enough to let them know that you
            were going to start taking care of yourself.

Although tentative at first, the woman gained confidence and
enthusiasm for the idea of disclosing a small part of the abuse she
suffered to just one person in the family.  After some lengthy
discussion, the woman decided that the safest person in the family
was an aunt on her mother's side.  The woman and the therapist
decided that her first call should simply disclose to the aunt that
she had some bad memories from childhood that had been causing
some upset.  In the next session, the woman was obviously pleased
with her efforts and the information she discovered.

WOMAN:      I called my aunt and told her that I was having
            bad memories about the past.  It was like I
            dropped a bomb!  My aunt didn't say nothing for
            about two minutes.  Then she said, "Oh, [the
            woman's name], I've always felt so bad about
            what happened to you kids.  Especially you."  I
            asked her what happened, and she told me that
            she knew that I had been sexually abused by that
            man.  She said she told my mom not to let me
            stay there any more but that my mom didn't
            believe her.  She said there were a lot of bad
            things that happened to us kids.
THERAPIST:  How does that make you feel?
WOMAN:      (*smiling*)  For the first time in my life I think I'm
            not crazy.

The independent confirmation of the sexual abuse and the injustice that surrounded the woman's childhood gave her a perspective on the family that was impossible for the therapist to give. She knew that she was abused and that somehow she was not "crazy," but the aunt's acknowledgment of the abuse credited the woman and confirmed that she was indeed entitled to pain. This initial phone call by the woman truly let the cat out of the bag. Within two days, the aunt had called the woman's sisters to unload some of her own disturbing memories about the past and indicated to them that the woman had initiated the call. Three of the sisters then called the woman directly and started sharing their own legacies of the abuse. Even though these discussions digressed into some blaming, the support the woman felt reduced her pain as she felt her siblings express care and concern. This convinced the woman she was on the right track.

In the next two sessions, the therapist and the woman talked about anger associated with the sexual abuse, desertion by her father, abandonment by her mother, and upset concerning her two children who were adopted. The focus of the therapy was to try to make the protective changes in the family system that were necessary without letting the situation drift into destructive blaming. The woman was quite willing to be coached and focused her anger in efforts to change the family for the better. Even though the abuse she suffered was now confirmed in the family, the woman felt the need to get answers directly from her parents.

WOMAN:     I just want to get some answers from my mom and dad. I want to know why she would leave me with those people. I want to know why my dad just acted like we were dead.

THERAPIST: Do you need to tell them anything?

WOMAN:     I just want to know. I'm really not that angry. I really know that Mom loved us. She was just not able to handle it. I'm really not sure about my dad. I just want them to know that I know that something happened and I'm getting better.

THERAPIST: It's like if you tell them you know what happened, you don't have to be quiet ever again.
You won't be alone.

WOMAN:     Right.  But I don't know if I can tell my mom.
She's not in such good health and I don't want to
hurt her.  My aunt told me not to tell her.

THERAPIST: Even though your aunt knows it happened?  Why
would your aunt tell you such a thing?

WOMAN:     She doesn't think my mom will believe me.  She
doesn't want everybody to get upset.  She doesn't
want to see me get hurt.

THERAPIST: You know the chances are good that your mother
won't believe you.  She may even get defensive
and angry at you.

WOMAN:     I know that.  I've thought about that.  Even with
talking to my aunt and my sisters I sometimes
still think maybe I'm not remembering it right.

THERAPIST: (*after a long pause*)  What do you think?

WOMAN:     It happened.  I'm not angry at anyone except the
man [who sexually abused her], but I need for
them to know that it did happen.

THERAPIST: And so what if you tell your mother and ask her
questions and everyone gets mad at you.

WOMAN:     They will just have to be mad.  I need to get on
with my life and all I want is some answers.  I'm
not wrong in just wanting that am I?

THERAPIST: It sounds to me like you just want them to know
that things will always be different and you won't
keep family secrets anymore.

It was clear to the therapist that the woman was going to
eventually speak directly to the mother about the sexual abuse.
She had connected very well with the perspective that if she took
care of herself, she could better take care of her children, and

especially her daughter. The support from the sisters and aunt was important, but it was evident that the aunt did not want to upset the family too much. The woman overtly expressed her resolve to get some answers and perhaps covertly expressed that she was determined to change how the family handled her in the future. However, in the rest of the session the woman expressed much hesitancy about speaking directly to her mother. The therapist suggested that an intermediate step might be to talk to her father first. The woman at first thought this was an impossibility because she did not know for sure where her father lived. While at the therapist's office, she made two phone calls that confirmed that he was still living in the area she thought. After she got the telephone number from information and there was some discussion focusing on keeping the conversation as constructive as possible, the session ended. The woman came to the next session reporting on the conversation with her father.

WOMAN:     My aunt called me before I made the call to my father. She said she didn't want me to be surprised if he wouldn't talk to me. I called anyway. We had a good conversation. At first it wasn't so good because I could tell he was really thrown off guard. But then I told him that I was having some bad memories of the past. He told me that things were bad and that he just tried to go on with life. He said the past was really painful for him.

THERAPIST: Was he specific about what was painful?

WOMAN:     No. I could tell he knew some of the things I was talking about and I didn't want to push it too much. He just said that things were really bad for all of us. I asked him why we never heard from him after he left. He said that he and my mom had so much trouble that he just figured it would be better if he didn't come by. I told him that we wanted to see him. Then he told me after

he married again he just didn't think it was right.
He did ask me some questions though.  I was
shocked!

THERAPIST: What did he ask you?

WOMAN:     He asked me about me and my kids.  He was
sorry that I got divorced.  And then he told me
something that blew me away.  He said that if I
ever needed any help I could call him.

THERAPIST: What do you think about that?

WOMAN:     I think he means it.  There is very little he would
do because he's still married and has another
family.  But I asked him if I could write him and
he said he would like that.

The woman displayed an incredible amount of insight in
handling the conversation with her father.  While effectively
changing the family system by contacting him, she sensed that she
could not become too specific about her painful memories.  She
connected with the lost and abusive father in a constructive
manner, opening some possibilities of relationship instead of
living with a vague recollection of the damage the man had caused.
While she realized that there would be limited connection with
and perhaps little help from the father in reality, the insight
enabled her to change her perspective and protect herself from the
damaging memories of the father.

The woman was so bolstered by the conversation with the father
that she was now more enthusiastic about discussing the sexual
abuse directly with her mother.  After role-playing several
possible scenarios of the conversation with the therapist, the
woman decided she would call her mother during the week.  In
the next session the woman discussed her conversation with her
mother.

WOMAN:     I talked to her for about an hour.  I told her what
I remembered about the sexual abuse.  She said

that she just couldn't believe that about that
couple.

THERAPIST: How did that make you feel?

WOMAN: I wasn't surprised. I knew it would be real hard
for her to hear that. It was hard for me to say. I
finally just took a deep breath and told her.

THERAPIST: Was she defensive? Did she get mad at you?

WOMAN: I don't think she was mad at me. It was like she
was just shocked. She kept saying that she just
couldn't believe that happened. I told her that
even if she didn't believe me, it happened. And I
told her that part of my upset all these years was
holding things inside and I wasn't going to do
that any more. I told her I was getting help.

THERAPIST: How are you?

WOMAN: I wish she would have believed me.


Certainly the interchange between the woman and her mother
would have been more constructive had the two been able to come
to some agreement about the sexual abuse. Through the next
several weeks, the woman reported that she had two more
conversations with her mother. Although the mother never
accepted any responsibility for possible relational damage from
the woman's childhood, the interchanges were reported to be
constructive. The woman stated that her mother was warmer
toward her and was taking more of an interest in her.

What is clear from this case is that even though the woman did
not have a restoration and healing of relationships with her family,
insight had allowed her to escape the emotional damage the family
had caused. The family had simply lost much of the power to
perpetuate any of the emotional trauma that was initiated in the
woman's childhood. The woman had the insight that enabled her
to protect herself and take better control of her life. Toward the
end of therapy, her physical symptomatology was almost completely alleviated, and she reported that she was doing much better

as a parent. Several months later, she started accessing skill-training workshops to prepare her to continue her education.

In this case, the work of forgiveness was carried as far as was possible at the time. For whatever reasons, the meager resources of the mother and father limited their abilities to restore the relationship with the woman. But the damage from the past had been specified and addressed enough that the woman was clear that she was now free from the old relationships that made her a victim. Insight allowed her to better control her life and make a clearer and more constructive intergenerational contribution for the sake of herself and her children. In many instances, this insight is as much forgiveness as a family is able to achieve. But the possibilities in this case are encouraging. Since the damaging family system had now significantly changed, the woman knew how to protect herself and ensure that interactions would either be trustworthy or not take place. Since the family, for the most part, was able to tolerate the change and not become more intense and destructive, the possibility of future expressions of love and trust between the woman and her parents existed. In this family, as with many others, insight may be only the first station along the road to more work of forgiveness in the future.

*Chapter Eight*

# CLINICAL APPLICATION OF UNDERSTANDING

*with*
*William T. Anderson, Ed.D.*

I t was a stirring scene. In 1981, Pope John Paul II had been shot by a Turkish radical by the name of Ali Agca in an assassination attempt. Less than a year later in a private room in the prison, there sat the Pope with the very man who had attempted to kill him. Private words were exchanged between the two, but the Pope was reported to make an effort to forgive the would-be assassin. As he sat face to face with the Pope, Agca was in a very different position than he was on the day he wielded the deadly pisol, firing wildly from a crowd that was gathered. Sitting in the prison in relative isolation with the man he shot, he was benign and powerless to do any more harm. But more striking than the absence of power was the compassion that was evident between the two men. As they sat with one another, they appeared not as Pope and terrorist, but as two real men. Power was diffused, and

William T. Anderson, Ed.D., is Associate Professor, Department of Family Sciences, Texas Women's University, Denton, Texas.

identification was made. This in essence is the work of exonerating people who have done us unjustified harm. The victimizer's
power to do more harm is gauged and monitored by the victim in
the station of insight, but the tough work of identification is found
in the second station of understanding.

In Chapter Three, the second station of forgiveness, the work
of understanding, was discussed. This involves two primary tasks
for the victim. The first task is to identify the injustices that the
victimizer experienced in the past and make personal identification with the victimizer. This process enables the victim to
exonerate the victimizer of evil intent. In turn, this allows the
victim to become free from internalized rage, usually of long
duration. The second task for the victim is to acknowledge the
difficult issue of the responsibility of the victimizer; despite the
victimizer's own personal trauma, the victimizer is still responsible for his or her own actions. The work of these first two tasks
then serves to relieve the victim of the burden of shame and pain
that occurred long ago. Now in the present, the victim can see that
he or she is a lovable person.

## CASE EXAMPLE, PART ONE:
## REOPENING THE FAMILY COFFIN

This type of understanding in the work of forgiveness is
sometimes difficult to achieve because of the complexity of
empathizing with one's victimizer while still holding him or her
accountable for the unjustified action. As in so much of life, the
dual nature of exoneration demands that the victim maintain
balance. On one hand, victims must understand that they might
be capable of causing the same unfair damage if they were in a
circumstance similar to that of the victimizer. On the other, the
victims must understand that the injustice indeed caused damage
for which the victimizer is responsible regardless of the past
circumstances or family backgrounds. The therapist working
with an individual or family in the station of understanding must

therefore be willing to shift the therapeutic leverage in an oscillating fashion between this empathy and responsibility.

In the following case example, a 78-year-old widow who experienced periodic depression was placed in a personal care facility. The woman had a substantial loss of sight, which contributed to her need to seek additional care and services. The client had two adult children and three grandchildren. The two children—a 38-year-old daughter and a 36-year-old son—were both married and lived in the city where the personal care facility was located. Her adult children became frustrated with the mother's depression and her lack of effort in adjusting to her new surroundings. Family members would have severe arguments, resulting in both mother and children accusing one another of insensitivity and lack of understanding.

Using the techniques of life validation and life review (Hargrave & Anderson, 1992), the therapist met alone with the widow for four sessions. The woman revealed very little information concerning her childhood because she said she could not remember. She divorced her husband after 21 years of marriage because he had an affair with another woman. The widow recalled vast amounts of specific information about her career as a working woman; however, when asked about her children's growing-up years, she gave sketchy information because she said she could not remember.

Since the woman seemed to be selective in her memory loss, the therapist hypothesized that either the families of origin and of procreation were disengaged, or there was emotional pain in the past requiring her to repress some of her own history. The therapist decided to ask the two adult children to participate in helping the mother in therapy.

They quickly revealed a high level of hostility toward the mother, recalling her alcoholism and their unhappy home life as children. The mother denied ever having a problem with drinking, stating that she had abstained from alcohol for the past eight years. The son said that talking about all these issues from the past was like "re-opening the family coffin. There it still is, the same old crud."

During the first family session, the therapist tried to maintain a position of multidirected partiality, both to the efforts of the mother in raising her children as a single parent and to the plight of the children growing up.

THERAPIST: Tell me what it was like for all of you growing up.
SON: The pits. *(The daughter nods in agreement.)*
THERAPIST: What was it like?
SON: Basically, all I remember was her being drunk every weekend. Foul mouthed. Not the kind of person you would want to be around.
THERAPIST: Who raised you?
SON: We basically raised ourselves.

After some discussion among the siblings about the fast food that their mother often fed them and their search for nurturing in other families, the daughter summed it up: "It was no good. It certainly was not pleasant."

THERAPIST: It sounds hopeless.
DAUGHTER: It was. It was like—I remember thinking—after she would be drunk, it would always be the same pattern. She would get drunk. She might or might not come home. The next morning would be the apologies. It was always the same pattern.
SON: Yes. It would be: Here is the next apology letter.

From the opening few minutes of this first family session, it was clear to the therapist how profound were the distrust and destructive entitlement in the family. Each family member carried severe relational injury from the family. The siblings felt that they had not been nurtured and cared for as children and were bound together against their "problemed" mother.

Left powerless by the enormous charges that her children had
made against her, the mother responded with a meager defense,
which then produced further relational hurt and distrust.

THERAPIST: As you have heard your children talk about you,
what do you believe they are trying to communicate to you?

MOTHER: They don't give a damn about me.

THERAPIST: (*blocking the angry response from the children*)
Tell me how you believe they don't give a damn
about you.

MOTHER: It's just the way I feel. No matter what I say or
do, they just don't care about me.

The mother was very accurate in understanding the relational
reality of the family. She was so much of a scapegoat to her
children that she was unable to make it up to them. The mother
felt they did not care for her; the children, however, wanted her
to care for them, not vice versa. They retaliated with angry
accusations.

The children once again complained of the mother's drinking
and of her minimal nurturing of them as children. The therapist
then responded by supporting the adult children, in their complaints about the poor nurturing they received, and the mother,
who did the best she knew how as a single parent. This did not
satisfy the children, who pressed the mother to express remorse
and some apology for her poor parenting.

MOTHER: Well, I really don't know what they are talking
about. I am not trying to keep anything to myself
or say that I'm sorry because I really don't think
that I have anything to apologize for. The past is
the past—I don't think about the past. I don't feel
like I owe them an apology.

It was true that the two children had an impoverished childhood, growing up with an alcoholic mother. However, the mother herself came from a love-starved family of origin. Then she was deserted by her husband and left to fend for herself and her two dependent children. The mother's pain and struggle were substantial. Indeed, she had raised her children the best she knew how, under very stressful circumstances.

In the next session, only the daughter chose to attend. This seemed to indicate that the son viewed the therapy effort as useless. During this session, the therapist tried to extend partiality to both the mother and the daughter. He did this by telling the daughter that the mother did indeed owe the children the care and nurturing that they did not receive when they were young. In addition, he supported the mother by maintaining that she did not receive care and nurturing when she was a little girl.

THERAPIST: I think you are a good, strong woman. But I
           don't think you know how to give affection
           because you have not had it yourself.
MOTHER:    I don't know.
THERAPIST: Where do you think your mother should get this?
DAUGHTER: I see three possibilities: God, herself, and you.
           Maybe a combination of all three.
THERAPIST: Would you accept it from somebody outside the
           family like me?
MOTHER:    All help is appreciated.
THERAPIST: It's not help. It is what you are owed.

The therapist was correct that the mother was owed affection. However, he overestimated his ability to give these things to the mother. The therapist could coach the mother toward initial giving steps, but he could not satisfy familial obligations to a family to which he did not belong. The woman and her children had to find and utilize their own resources, to build a slow gradient of giving to one another; these resources could not come from the therapist.

Both adult children attended the next family session. The therapist, through the use of imagery, had the mother visualize her own mother comforting her when she was in pain as a little girl. He then asked the daughter if she would be comfortable with her mother doing that with her.

The daughter was willing to accept this gesture of love from the mother. Through this imaging, the mother was able to imagine how she could communicate love and care to the daughter, who in turn accepted this gesture from her mother. The family began to experience some hope.

In the next session, the adult children gave some signs that there was hope that old, unresolved family issues could be addressed. The therapist then asked the children to reveal childhood hurts that they wished the mother to address. The daughter then recalled an incident that had occurred 20 years ago. She discovered her drunken mother in bed two different times on the same day with a different man each time.

THERAPIST: (*to the mother*) Did this happen?
MOTHER:    I do not remember it happening, but I guess that it did.
THERAPIST: I know that you don't remember, but it is time to take responsibility. Did it happen?
MOTHER:    I am sure that it did.
THERAPIST: What do you believe that would have done to your daughter when she was a little girl?
MOTHER:    It probably scared her to death.

The therapist then directed the mother to apologize to the daughter on bent knees, which she did willingly. Yet the mood in the session shifted from hope to mild despair. Although the mother made a legitimate effort, the son sensed that her heart was not in the apology. The family was just beginning to locate resources, but the therapist pushed them too hard, draining energy from the family members.

THERAPIST: How do you all feel?

SON:      It just feels like she is not taking responsibility or
          blame. It seems like it is not sinking into her
          what she has done. She says she doesn't remem-
          ber or she is drunk.

In the next session, the therapist encouraged the son to express
his expectations of the mother. This intervention seemed to be a
mistake: He asked the mother to dip into her meager pool of
resources, rather than helping the whole family to identify the
family resources. The therapist was not being partial to the
mother's side of the family intergenerational ledger; rather, he
became part of the accusing coalition of the adult children against
the mother.

SON:      Well, who in the world would want to be around
          someone who is as negative as you are?

MOTHER:   No one. I'm not asking for anyone to be with
          me. I cannot help the way I think.

SON:      You've got a problem. You've got to work on
          helping yourself.

MOTHER:   I have got a helluva problem.

The mother was placed in a no-win situation. She was asked to
give love and affection, about which she knew so little. Then,
when she was unable to produce at the expectation level of the
children, she was chastised for her failure. Family energy began
to disintegrate during this session.

The therapist, still part of the children's coalition, asked the
mother to complete before the next family session three of four
tasks specifically requested by the adult children. He probably
should have required the adult children to recognize and validate
the mother's efforts to give to them.

The next (and last) family session revealed that the mother
completed one task and made an effort at another. These efforts

of hers clearly did not meet the expectations of either the adult children or the therapist. Her failure brought the mother to the point where she refused to continue with therapy.

MOTHER: I am so tired and weak. I have no interest. My body is tired and I don't feel like fooling around with this stuff.

THERAPIST: It takes a lot of energy to deal with this stuff. Do you want me to give you another opportunity?

MOTHER: I really don't want one, to be honest with you. It is not because I don't want to help my kids. I am very tired and very confused.

THERAPIST: You feel pounded down.

MOTHER: I really do. *(pauses and starts to cry)* I have prayed to God to take my life and put an end to my pain.

Here the mother expressed herself beautifully in her accurate description of the family situation. She wanted to help her children, but was confused about how to proceed. Every time the mother would make an effort, she felt battered by failure around resources she did not have. Like a boxer who had been pounded for fifteen rounds, she was so drained of energy that all she could do was to hope that the end would come soon. Family therapy ended with this session, without any significant lasting change in the family system.

## CASE EXAMPLE, PART TWO:
## CLOSING THE FAMILY COFFIN

Three years after the family terminated therapy, the adult daughter contacted the therapist to express her concern about her brother's marriage. The therapist considered this interest on the part of the sibling as an act of giving in the family system. At first, the brother participated in the therapy somewhat reluctantly.

However, in the third session, he stated clearly that he indeed wished to work on his relationship with his wife of 18 years. It was then agreed that the brother and his wife would come for marital therapy.

While the therapist was out of the room, consulting the team behind the mirror, the brother made this startling observation to his sister: "The whole thing that makes my marriage so terrible is that I know that we were unwanted by our mother. If we were not wanted, we were not loved. And that's what happened to that kid (referring to his own son)."

In a somewhat contented tone of voice, he then told his sister how his son occasionally gave him a hug and an "I love you." "It makes me feel so good." This father clearly wanted from his offspring what he did not get from his own mother. The cycle of destructive entitlement had continued.

## Marital Therapy

In the opening session of marital therapy, the brother told the therapist that he wanted his aging mother to express remorse for her not being present for him during his childhood. Yet the brother openly wondered how present he was now to his own son.

The marital therapy continued for several more sessions. The son participated in one of these sessions. It was during this same time period that the mother of the two siblings (grandmother of the son) found out that she had serious heart deterioration, attributed to a lifelong habit of heavy smoking. It soon became clear that the mother had just a few months left to live.

## Intergenerational Therapy

Three years earlier, intergenerational family therapy focusing on the relationship between the mother and her adult children had reached an impasse. Taking a different approach this time, the therapist hypothesized that the dying mother and the daughter might be open to giving to the brother and his wife, as the couple worked to improve their marriage. With this in mind, the therapist scheduled an intergenerational family session that included the mother, her two adult children, and her son's wife. The therapeutic focus centered on the family members giving to the brother, with the hope that this would deepen the sense of both entitlement and obligation among all the family members.

*Session One.* Midway through the first family session, the mother stated with personal conviction: "God has forgiven me for what I have done wrong in the past." The clear implication was that her adult children present had not forgiven her.

THERAPIST: So that's why you don't fear death. You are ready to go. Earlier, your son asked what you feared.

MOTHER: Now I don't fear anything. I make the best of it.

THERAPIST: Some things can't be changed *(referring overtly to the heart condition and covertly to the children's refusal to forgive the mother before she died).*

MOTHER: I do the best I can. Day by day.

THERAPIST: That sounds like a gift for your son and his wife as they struggle together in their marriage. *(turning toward her son)* Who are you afraid of?

BROTHER: I'm not afraid of anything.

The wife immediately confronted her husband by recalling how he had expressed to her that he was scared of what was happening in their relationship. He responded by saying that he was frustrated, not scared. The sister then also confronted her brother about her observing his fear of not being loved and of his wife's possibly divorcing him. This exchange also brought an immediate denial from the brother.

The therapy had now moved to the level of the family anxiety, rooted in each member's fear of not having been or being loved. Denial of this anxiety ran deep in this family system. Distance from one another served to protect the family members from this painful issue. As the mother's health deteriorated and her death drew closer, the level of the family anxiety increased. Soon there would be no more time left to settle the unresolved issues between the dying mother and her adult children. This tension now manifested itself during the therapy session in another part of the intergenerational family system, namely, the brother's marriage.

The brother acknowledged that his wife might divorce him. He likened marriage to a job: if this one doesn't work out, move on to another! This remark brought an immediate response from all the other family members, who professed astonishment about his viewing intimate ties in such a perfunctory manner. Yet each one of them seemed to feel the same about the intergenerational family ties in their family of origin.

THERAPIST: (*to the couple*) If you were both to die tomorrow, what would you like to tell each other right now?

BROTHER: (*to the therapist*) I would tell her that I love her.

THERAPIST: How about telling her right now.

BROTHER: (*to his wife, followed by nervous laughter*) I love you and I would miss you.

WIFE: I love you, too.

At this point, the sister put her finger in her mouth, signalizing regurgitation. All of the family members laughed nervously. The therapist then confronted the family members on how they found it difficult to accept emotional closeness and how they used humor to fend off the intimacy.

SISTER: That's true. We want closeness, but we don't want the vulnerability.

At this stage in the session, the therapist then posed to the adult children a question similar to the one given to the couple.

THERAPIST: If this were your mother's last day, what would each of you want to tell her right now, face-to-face?

BROTHER:   (*directly to mother*) I hope you find peace now.

SISTER:    (*directly to mother*) The last few months we have talked out a lot of things. I love you.

MOTHER:    (*to sister, as she strokes her hand*) I love you, too, babe.


It was clear during this session that the family members were having trouble with closeness. They all used humor to hide the deep hurt and unfinished business that tended to keep each family member at a distance from the others. This family session ended without much progress in this area. The mother felt forgiven by God, but not by her adult children. The adult children remained distant from their mother, who they felt had not loved and nurtured them when they were children.


*Session Two.* One month later the family met again. The son of the brother participated in this session, along with the mother, the brother and his wife, and the sister. This session took place just five weeks before the mother's death from heart failure.

Family anxiety about her approaching death became clearly evident at the start of the session. All the adult family members began talking about a plane crash in another state; this accident claimed the lives of several acquaintances of the sister. The sister then mentioned two relatives who had cancer; however, no one brought up the mother's serious condition. The therapist then spoke directly to the mother about her serious illness and her present state of health. Her response again was that she was living day by day.

Later in the session, the family discussed the birthday of the grandson. At this point, the mother gave her grandson a birthday card and money, another sign of her trying to give to her son by reaching out to his son. The therapist took this opportunity to ask the mother to give more to her grandson.

THERAPIST: How can you help your grandson learn to let go of things that don't work out?

MOTHER:   (*to grandson*)  Stand up for yourself; don't follow the crowd.

GRANDSON: What about drugs and smoking?  [*The grandson was aware that the mother smoked and drank heavily, at least in the past.*]

MOTHER:   Don't do them and you won't know what you are missing.

This reaching out by the mother seemed effective, since at the break in the therapy, the grandson gave the mother a warm embrace, a rare experience in this distant intergenerational family. This intimate exchange took place in front of his parents, who chose to ignore this rare moment of intergenerational closeness.

Later in the session, the therapist apologized to the mother because earlier in the session he had made a light reference to her fatal disease. He then self-disclosed about a close brush with death he had 30 years earlier when he had a serious illness.

MOTHER:   (*to therapist*)  I don't have anybody to talk to or tell.

This sounded like her anger at her adult children, who continued to maintain a distant, defensive position regarding their mother. She quickly focused this anger on the therapist by bluntly telling him that she could talk to her friends better than she could talk to the therapist.

THERAPIST: I admire your honesty... What I like about you is your willingness to come here, despite your serious illness, to help your son and his wife.

MOTHER: (*to therapist*) I want to do anything I can. It doesn't sound like they are so desperate that they can't work it out. I know they have problems, but I'm sure they can work them out. And God knows how I love my grandson; I love him to death.

This family session ended on a rather somber note. The mother, lonely as she faced her impending death, reached out in her own awkward manner to her adult children; she wanted and needed personal contact with them. For their part, the adult children responded by maintaining a distant, defensive position.

*Session Three*. In the next session, the intergenerational family met for the last time before the mother died ten days later. The adult children continued to express their complaints about the mother to the therapist, not directly to her. During this last session, the mother admitted her drinking patterns and apologized to her adult children. Apparently, they failed to acknowledge this rejunctive effort on the mother's part.

MOTHER: (*speaking to the group*) You are all so wonderful. You are all so wonderful.

THERAPIST: I have noticed that your mother is always so positive about each of you children.

SISTER: That's an interesting observation. She is always so negative about everything else, but not about us.

THERAPIST: Even though you didn't get what you wanted as children from your mother, maybe you can appreciate her now as an adult.

MOTHER: (*again, speaking to the entire group*) I don't

BROTHER:   bother them.  I let them lead their own lives.

BROTHER:   (*to therapist*)  We have come to peace with
                ourselves about mother.  Even after we left
                home, we'd visit her on weekends and she'd be
                drunk.

MOTHER:    I was a weekend drinker.

The  siblings then talked to the therapist about how they learned
to let go of expecting anything good from their mother.

BROTHER:   We have learned to blow off her negative atti-
                tudes and complaining. My wife and son take it
                more personal.

MOTHER:    I'm just awfully sorry.

At the end of this session, the son asked that his mother express
some remorse for not providing nurturing to them when they were
children many years ago. Neither of the adult children acknowledged the mother's admission in this family session that she was
a weekend drinker and that she was "awfully sorry." The adult
children agreed that in the next family session, they would be
prepared to celebrate the progress made in the brother's marital
relationship. However, they remained adamant that they could not
celebrate any improvement between them and their dying mother.

*Final Session.*   Three months after the mother's death, the
family met for a final session. Present were the sister, the brother
and his wife, and their son.   The members of the observing team
joined the family in the room. The sister explained how, since the
death of her mother, she had been able to be closer to her own
husband, who had also felt that his own mother did not love him.

THERAPIST: Did you know that your mother loved you?

SISTER:     Oh, yes.  The connection was when I all of a

sudden realized it after she died. We had that discussion here in therapy the last time, about how she always talked good about us. After her death, it sunk in that she truly loved us and did the best job she knew how. That's what made me able to forgive her. She did the best she could.

THERAPIST: Your mother had been saying that for a couple of years and nobody believed her.

SISTER: I know. That's right.

THERAPIST: How did you know that your mother truly loved you and truly did the best she could?

SISTER: It was that night of the last family session, when we all sat around here in her presence and discussed it. That's when it really clicked. It was like reading a book. Then, after her death, I reread the book and knew that she loved us.

BROTHER: That's what I said when we were in Mother's apartment after her funeral. Gosh, I remember thinking: If I only had five more minutes.

Later in the session, the therapist helped the brother and his wife to deal directly with each other, without their son coming between them, as he had done for the past several years. The son, now freed of the triangulation, was able to return to his age-appropriate role in the family.

During a break in the therapy, the brother was alone in the therapy room. His sister reentered the therapy room, immediately went over to him and gave him a warm embrace.

SISTER: I love you.

BROTHER: I love you, too.

SISTER: I just find it incredible that the cycle continues to go on.

The second station in forgiveness involves three tasks in the internalized work of understanding. The victim needs to identify the injustices experienced, to acknowledge the responsibility of the victimizer, and to release the burden of shame and pain that occurred long ago. The clinical case just presented offers a good illustration of this station.

The adult children in this family had very clearly identified the injustices that they suffered at the hands of their mother when they were small children. Their mother had provided food, clothes, and shelter, but not much more. They felt deprived of security, love, acceptance, and nurturance; their pain was deep.

In the course of the therapy, they slowly began to understand the many hurts and lacks in their mother's life. This enabled them to exonerate her of evil intention. As the sister noted, "She did the best she could." In turn, this enabled all of them, in varying degrees, to let go of their long-term rage at not being nurtured and loved. They had come to understand the relational and emotional field of their family of origin.

Both of them openly acknowledged the responsibility of the mother. The brother remarked that "... we were not wanted, and if we are not wanted, we are not loved." They began to understand the family transactions between them and their mother. The brother even wondered how this same pattern of not being loved was being repeated in his own family of procreation, where he did not want or love his own son.

As they began to empathize with their mother, and understand her personality and motivations, they began to let go of their shame and pain as neglected children. In varying degrees, they began to realize that their mother's neglect of them as children was rooted in herself and in her own past; it had nothing to do with their own goodness. Three months after the mother's death, the sister put it so clearly: "After her death, it sunk in that she truly loved us and did the best job she knew how. That's what made me able to forgive her. She did the best she could." These adult children now began to realize that they were and are lovable persons.

*Chapter Nine*

# CLINICAL APPLICATION OF GIVING THE OPPORTUNITY FOR COMPENSATION

Sometimes I am amazed at the valiant efforts people make in the work of forgiveness associated with past family pain. People are so tied to their intergenerational families, wanting and seeking loving and trustworthy relationships, that they are often willing to make powerful commitments to see the relationships restored. They keep trying and believing that the process of forgiveness can make their family relationships better for themselves and for their children. This commitment and effort toward restoration are often made in the face of past or even present heinous actions that would seem insurmountable to many of us. Such is the power of the intergenerational family. People know that making things right with their intergenerational past will have a direct effect on the posterity of the entire family.

Intergenerational relationships, however, are not the only ties many of us have to families. Many of us have spouses with whom we have sought to make a relationship through spoken promises as opposed to blood lineage. Most have friendships in which love and trust are so strong that they transcend acquaintance and familiarity to a lifelong bond that is like a family bond, even though there may be no official legal or social connection. Even in larger systems, there are arguments to be made that we are members of companies, organizations, communities, nations, and the world, and that these relationships somehow tie us together in a group that can loosely be called family.

Ties to these types of "family" relationships may not be as clear as in the intergenerational framework, but many have made just as powerful commitments to love and trust in these relationships as they have to the families from which they came. Since these *horizontal* family relationships are also built on love and trust, they are likewise vulnerable to unjustified damage in the balance of obligations and entitlements. But just as we are vulnerable in horizontal relationships to unjustified damage and sometimes unbearable hurts, we also have the opportunity to restore these relationships through the work of forgiving.

In the two stations involved with forgiving, we essentially reopen the book on the violation to the place where the damage occurred and allow our victimizer an opportunity to give us the love and trust we deserved. Whether the relationship is horizontal (friends, spouses, siblings) or vertical (intergenerational: grand-parents, parents, children), forgiving can result in *healing* rela-tionships. As mentioned before, however, this potential healing is bought at an enormous cost. In order to be healed, we must become vulnerable to the very people who caused the damage. In the third station, giving the opportunity for compensation, the victim does risk vulnerability  to the person who caused the damage, but the risk is mitigated by acts of love and trustworthi-ness over a period of time. As trustworthiness is proven to the victim, the victim becomes more and more willing to be vulnerable to restoring the damaged relationship.

## CASE EXAMPLE:
## ENTERING BACK IN IS RISKY BUSINESS

It is essential to remember that tremendous hurt and damage in a family can be perpetuated by real or even by *perceived* violations in the ethical balance of love and trust. Victims of this real or perceived type of hurt and damage may internalize the violation into severe shame or externalize it into anger or rage against the violator. In the case where an individual has been damaged by a family member, anger and rage may prevent the victim from ever reconciling with the victimizer. Such was the case in the following example. A 52-year-old woman and man were having severe marital difficulty. The couple had one grown male son who was married and had a successful career. The man, who had had paralysis from a stroke for 20 years, was a former banker. The woman, who had always stayed at home taking care of him and the son, allowed the man to manage all the financial resources and make all the decisions for the family. Dramatic evidence of the woman's rage toward the man and their destructive anger was frequently demonstrated by arguments such as the one that follows.

MAN:     (*very angry*) I can't believe you said that. How else more plainly can you say that you want me to die? You told me I should die!

WOMAN:     (*filled with rage*) I didn't say that! I said that you lived as if you were going to die and it didn't matter to you what we had to worry about or think about. And I'll tell you, I know you don't care about us. Every time I have to deal with your financial problems it is just one more blow—one more thing to show me how little you care. You didn't care for me or anybody around you!
I have had to deal with this all over again when I got this (*points to an envelope containing infor-*

*mation regarding their financial status*), I thought
to myself how little you cared.

MAN:        The tape is going over, and over, and over again!
            We aren't going to make any progress as long as
            you have that going.  That [information] is well
            over 20 years old.

WOMAN       That's right!  That's how long this has been going
            on.  It never stopped until I got a little money of
            my own.  But it's still going on.  Nothing in your
            life has ever stopped!
            It doesn't matter.  I'm the one who always has to
            give you all the care.  And with what?  Nothing!

MAN:        What do you mean?  I gave you everything I had.
            I did the best I could.

   The woman revealed early in the sessions that she had been
physically abused by both her mother and her father and that she
felt dominated by her family of origin.  She stated that she had
always blindly trusted her husband to take care of her because she
believed for many years that she was not competent to take care
of herself.  The couple came to therapy originally because the
woman was ready to divorce the man.  She was ready to take this
action after an incident involving the couple's son.  The son had
asked the mother to come and help out in his business for a few
weeks.  While the woman was out of town helping the son, the man
had called the son and suggested that he suspected the mother was
having an affair.  The son became concerned and confronted the
woman.  When the woman discovered the accusation from her
husband, she became enraged.  The man admitted that he had no
reason to believe that she was having an affair, but believed she
was slipping away from his control.

   It was discovered in the early therapy sessions that the woman
had a history of depressed behavior and had had three previous
hospitalizations.  The man had always been domineering in the
relationship and had intentionally manipulated the woman throughout their history together.  He revealed  that he had been the oldest

and favored child in his family of origin. He stated that his dominance was simply an expression of his father's belief about manhood.

After eight therapy sessions, the man came to regret the action he had taken against his wife and became concerned with the way he had neglected and manipulated her throughout the course of the marriage. At first, the woman did not believe the sincerity of his apology. Eventually she came to believe him more but stated that if she were to stay married to him there would have to be several changes in the relationship. The primary change was that she demanded to be in control of all the family and financial decisions. The man agreed to the condition. However, the woman quickly discovered that the man had made poor financial decisions throughout the course of their marriage. Because of his past decisions, she consistently questioned his care for her and the family.

It became apparent to the cotherapists in the case that, even though the woman recognized some of the man's efforts toward change, the original violation of telling the son that she had an affair assaulted her so that she felt the entire marriage was based on mistrust and manipulation. Her perceptions prevented relational progress. The damage she had experienced from childhood and the marriage created a climate where she consistently felt that the man was out to get her and hurt her again. She used her rage to keep her distance so she would not have to be vulnerable in the relationship. As a result, the slightest mistake on the man's part in his effort was considered to be a "same old story" transgression, and she would declare that the man was incapable of caring and would never change. She would not only become enraged about his current behavior, but also recount a litany of his previous domination and relational abuse. This made the marriage intolerable for both the man and the woman.

In this case, it was decided by the cotherapists that the station of giving the opportunity for compensation might be helpful in getting the couple to move past some of the manipulation and pain involved in the relationship, and create a new trust between the two. The first step in this process was to help the husband give to his wife by acknowledging his previous relational irresponsibility. Instead of talking about the marriage in terms of her duty as a wife, he was encouraged to talk about the marriage in terms of his love for her.

THERAPIST: You two have been married a long time. You have been through a lot together. The stroke—I wonder what it would have been like for you *(pointing to the man)* if you would have known you were going to have this problem. How would it have been to ask her to marry you if you would have known? What would you have said to her if you would have known what your life was going to be like, but you still wanted her to marry you?

MAN: I just don't think I could have asked her. Knowing what my life would have been like, I just don't think I could have asked her to go through that much.

THERAPIST: Go back to that October day when you asked her to marry you. What would you have said to her if you would have been privy to your life? What would you say if you knew what you know now?

MAN: I don't have the words.

THERAPIST: Give it a try *(pointing the man toward the woman)*.

MAN: *(long pause, looking toward the woman)* I am looking at a long road ahead of us. I would ask you to be with me along that road. I can't promise you happiness; I can't promise you prosperity; I can't promise you one thing. But I would ask you to marry me.

THERAPIST: Why would you ask her to marry you?

MAN: *(still looking at the woman)* I love you. I want you to be with me on this journey. I would ask

you to be with me on this journey but I don't
promise that it will be good.

THERAPIST: *(long pause)* What reason could you give her to
come along with you?

MAN: *(still looking at the woman)* The only real reason
I could give you is that I love you. I don't have
any question about that. I still think you are a
delight to be with, and I want to be with you.
Besides that, it's cold.
*(pause)* To be realistic, I would ask you to marry
me hoping that you would agree, but realistically
I don't think there would be any benefit in it for
you. It would just benefit me. I don't know that
I could offer you anything so that you would see
it being worthwhile for you.
I could offer a son. *(long pause)*

THERAPIST: You see how this is the same question now as it
was back on that October day? Basically then
you were asking her to accompany you on the
journey together. You're now further down the
road, but you are still asking her to be a partner
the rest of the way. But the reason that you ask
her now, the only real thing you have to offer her
is that you love her. There is nothing that really
benefits her. You don't have much to offer
except your love for her.

MAN: That's very true. I know that.

THERAPIST: How would it have been for you, if after that type
of proposal back in 1948—knowing that you
would have the stroke and paralysis—she would
have looked at you and said yes.

MAN: *(obviously touched)* I would have been about as
emotional as I am right now. I would feel happy
and very thankful.
*(long pause)* I would be so happy that she would
consent to be a part of my life knowing that it is a

> mess.  I can't picture a woman who would be
> willing to be in a relationship with a man with all
> my problems.
>
> THERAPIST: Well, let me help you try to picture her.  She is
> right there (*pointing toward the woman as the
> man nods in agreement*).  Because that is what
> she does right now—today.

There is little doubt that the stroke and paralysis had caused the man to be dependent upon the woman for years.  In his past manipulative and domineering position, it is doubtful that he ever expressed the gratitude and care for the woman that he had in the session.  The cotherapists were hopeful that this heartfelt expression from the man would have a twofold result.  First, it was hoped that the man would recognize his wife's commitment and sacrifice in caring for him not only in the past, but in the present.  This understanding would perhaps assist him in being more responsible in the present relationship.  Second, it was hoped that the man's declaration of love and thankfulness would be recognized by the woman as his partiality for her side of the marriage.  Many times, this type of credit given by a family member will be experienced as a trustworthy effort and resources in the family will increase.

Although the man seemed quite sincere in his effort to declare his feelings and credit the woman, the woman was not receptive.  She expressed her extreme doubt that the man meant what he said and that he would ever be a responsible marriage partner.  This was profound evidence of the relational deterioration and lack of trust that characterized the marriage.

> WOMAN:    I'm really to the place where I just don't believe
> he ever will change.  He has no intention of
> changing.  It is no fun to talk to somebody who
> never acknowledges you.  He only has one
> intention and that is to achieve his end.  There is
> never any give on his part to anyone else.
> All I hear is a hum of a voice.  That is what life

THERAPIST:      is like with him.  I don't even hope for any change.  I have none.

THERAPIST: Try to focus a moment on what he is asking.

WOMAN:     All he is asking me to do is to stay and take care of him.  I have said that I will stay and take care of him.

THERAPIST: No doubt that is part of it.  But maybe part of it is he is asking for an emotional relationship.

WOMAN:     Well, if he is, he could try to meet that emotional side.  I think he is just wanting to be cared for.

THERAPIST: That may be true, but I think you at least need to address this emotional question.

WOMAN:     The question is, will I meet his emotions?  The question is, will he meet mine?  If I tell him that I'm depressed, he gets on the phone or starts writing somebody trying to send me somewhere.  Just to tell him what I feel makes me feel better.  But instead of just being a person that will listen, he is off trying to send me somewhere.

The session ended with the woman very doubtful of the man's ability to change or sincerity about wanting to.  When there is prolonged relational damage as there was in this marriage, building any trustworthy effort is difficult.  The therapist must move carefully but consistently in helping the victim be willing to accept effort on the part of the victimizer.  In this case, willingness included the woman's acknowledgment that the man even *could* change.  After willingness to accept change and effort is established, the therapeutic effort in this station must center on keeping the expectations and efforts realistic.  This realism usually involves small efforts of trustworthy exchange at first, building to more substantial trustworthy interactions.

There was little doubt that much of the man's compassion was centered around the need he had for a caretaker.  However, since his effort seemed to be successful in helping him acknowledge the contribution and sacrifice his wife had made and seemed to make him more appreciative of her, the cotherapists asked the man to consider this question on whether he should ask the woman to make more sacrifice by staying married to him. The next session, the man returned with a typed letter recapping his thoughts on the question.

MAN:    Now concerning the question of whether I would ask my wife to still marry me as I did in 1948 if I knew I would have a stroke. I have thought about this answer for over a week.

I spent a full day typing answers. None of which satisfied me. I have learned that love should look for the best for the beloved. If I would have known then all of the physical problems and all of its unhappiness in my future, then I should have released [her name] from the understanding that we would marry.

I know now, that I didn't really know what love was back then. I do know that I loved you. I realize that my sexual desire for you, rather than mature love was dominant then. Yet, I did honestly want only you. I did then, just as I do now. I do not believe that I would have been big enough to cut out plans to marry you back then, even though I probably should have for your best interests. I was selfish and possessive back then just as I am now. But I believe that I am better now. I do love you, but I know better now what love actually is. I want the best for you now. I want you to have rest and as you requested, breathing room. I am offering to go to a care facility or to stay in a separate part of the house for as long as you need.

WOMAN:    (*after a pause, she responds fairly angrily*) It just doesn't seem very practical. You see, you have torn up what we had together. We don't have anything together.

MAN:      How can everything between us be wiped away?
WOMAN:    What you did wiped it all away.


The woman is extremely tentative about accepting any direct effort on the part of the man to change. This is understandable in that she had been in the marriage for several decades and been subject to tremendous injustice. As evidenced in the session, the effort on the man's part to directly express love and trustworthy effort to the woman stirred a tremendous amount of pain that she was unable to overcome. Therefore, the result of these efforts was a sense of hopelessness between the two. The cotherapists were aware of the very real possibility that the man's mixed motives of love and need for care could result in additional damage to the relationship. Unable to coach the woman on realistic expectations about the man's efforts and to clearly delineate the risks involved with his motives for the efforts, the cotherapists decided that perhaps the man could demonstrate trustworthy and unselfish giving to the intergenerational framework.

Both the man and the woman reported that the man had demonstrated these same selfish characteristics in the family. He stated that he had never had any interest in his grandchildren, and in fact could not recall their names. The woman criticized him heavily for his lack of nurturing of and care for the grandchildren. The cotherapists decided that effort toward the grandchildren offered the opportunity for the man to demonstrate his trustworthy and loving effort in a way that did not put the woman at risk. This gave the man the opportunity for compensation while further minimizing the risk of potential damage to the woman.

The cotherapists expressed this intention openly in the session so the woman would know why the man was shifting his effort to give from her to the grandchildren. They requested that he make contact with each of the grandchildren in some special manner such as writing a letter, telling old family stories, or giving away a token of his that they would find interesting. In the next session, the mood of the couple was distinctly less stressed.

THERAPIST: Now what did you bring here?

MAN:      (*reaching into a pile of knickknacks*) A whole
          bunch of stuff. My wife and I picked all this out.
          Here is an old key on a necklace—I'm not sure
          what that is.

Therapist: Did you used to wear it?

MAN:      No, I don't think so. But this, my wife gave me
          while we were in high school. It's an old belt
          buckle. This is a college ring. It was my
          college ring.
          Here is a baseball medal from when I was in high
          school.

THERAPIST: (*holding up the belt buckle*) Who would you give
          this to?

MAN:      I really had not planned. One of the girls I
          guess.

The man's lack of clarity about the tokens as well as his
confusion over which grandchildren would receive the tokens may
have been evidence of several things. The man may have been so
disconnected from the grandchildren for so many years that the
effort did not make much sense to him or he may have been
confused about exactly what to do. Another possibility was that
the man was truly disinterested in the grandchildren and was not
willing to make a loving and trustworthy effort toward them. But
as the session continued, it was clear that both the woman and the
man had worked together on the project. Later in the session, the
woman revealed some of her own memorabilia.

WOMAN:    (*holding a silver tray*) When my grandmother
          died, I pleaded with my mother for this tray. I
          really never knew why. I came across it when
          we were looking for all the other things. Look
          what is on it. (*The tray was embossed with a
          small girl on a swing.*)

> I didn't put this together until just the other day,
> but look. *(She takes out a picture of herself when
> she was a small girl on a similar swing.)* That
> dress is the only one my mother made me. It was
> beautiful. I never put those two things together.
> It made me cry. It makes me cry now.

Even though the man clearly was not too involved in making an effort toward the grandchildren at the beginning of the session, the woman was very involved with the exercise and had made a tremendous psychological connection with her past. Her connection was probably multifaceted, but it did indicate to the cotherapists the intensity of the woman's interest in connecting with the grandchildren and the feeling that the communication of love and trust to them had the possibility of affecting her current emotional field.

As the woman passed around the tray and the picture, the man picked up the woman's interest in endeavor and became more energetic in talking about connection with the grandchildren. Therefore, the cotherapists asked the man to continue the effort toward the grandchildren so that his faithful effort toward the grandchildren might be interpreted by the woman as an indication that he was capable of love and trust. In the next session, the man revealed some of his efforts to reach out toward the grandchildren. The woman gladly joined in this effort, and the two recounted several stories about their family.

MAN:       I wrote a letter today to one of my grandchildren.
THERAPIST: Who was it that you wrote today?
MAN:       I wrote [name of the child]. I sent him a picture
           of me and [woman's name] on horses back when
           we were in high school. I told him a story about
           us and the way we used to ride those horses. My
           horse's name was Prince and her horse's name
           was Bob.

THERAPIST: *(laughing)*  Very symbolic.

MAN:     *(also laughing)* Yes.  Anyway, I had a long conversation with him about how much we enjoyed riding and how we rode in the parade of the rodeo.  I thought it was a good letter.  It will take a while for him to understand it, but I think he will like it.

THERAPIST: How old is he?

MAN:     He's three, just about four.

WOMAN:    But this child is our little cowboy.  Last time I was there, he wouldn't go to bed without his cowboy boots on.

THERAPIST: *(laughing again)*  He wore his boots to bed?

WOMAN:    Absolutely.  That's how much he loves being a cowboy.

THERAPIST: I'm from Texas.  God bless that little boy's soul.

MAN:     *(laughing)*  That is why I wanted to write him and tell him that his grandmother and his granddaddy wore boots and rode horses.  I sent him that picture and told the story that on that day we rode downtown in a parade for the rodeo.  Now I don't know that it was exactly on that day, but I thought it would help him identify with the picture more.  So I felt like it was a fairly decent letter.

WOMAN:    *(after a pause)*  He is such a special little boy. He just loves those cowboy boots.  I remember we were out last year and they had him in a cute little sailor suit.  He cried and cried because he wanted to wear his cowboy boots.  You know, he cried so much that he finally got to wear those cowboy boots with that sailor's outfit.
That's just the way he is, so I told [man's name] that.  I suggested to him that since he liked to ride so much that this might be a way to connect to [the grandchild's name].

The man was now clearly getting involved with the effort to express loving care toward his grandchildren. The woman's effort to help the man identify with the grandchildren as well as her own identification with him showed her willingness to accept his efforts as evidence of love and trust toward the family as a whole. As she accepted this effort and he proved trustworthy in the effort, the emotional status of the relationship shifted. The woman was receiving the love and trust, albeit indirectly through the grandchildren, that she longed for and deserved. As she gained some of this entitlement, her anger and rage were greatly reduced and the two became involved in an intimate endeavor to care for the grandchildren.

Later in the same session, the cotherapists sought to expand the positive effect of the couple's effort. In an effort to build realism and commitment to the communication with the grandchildren, the cotherapists suggested that the man keep a copy file of all the letters, pictures, and memorabilia he sent to the grandchildren.

THERAPIST: Maybe you could photocopy all the letters you send.

MAN: That's a good idea. That way I could remember who I told what.

COTHERAPIST: You could look at it sort of like a diary that you keep of your relationship with your grandchildren. It will help you and your wife keep track of what was going on at what time.

WOMAN: You know that's true. His mother and my mother both kept all our letters. It's interesting to go back and read the trivia we wrote. Things I forgot. It is pleasant to go back and read those types of things. You're documenting something that you have done and felt.
*(looking toward her husband)* Maybe we could read some of those old letters and it would jog some more memories for us to tell.

MAN:        Maybe it would.  That picture certainly spurred a
            lot of memories in me and made it possible for
            me to write [the grandchild's name].  The picture
            and you telling me about how much he loved
            those boots!  I think that letter will probably be
            meaningful to him.
WOMAN:      Oh, he'll love it.  That's all he likes to think
            about is riding horses.

When the loving effort toward the grandchildren is contrasted
with the effort toward direct giving to the woman, one can see how
much relational progress was made in a short period of time.  The
man had violated the trustworthy balance of his relationship with
the woman in many ways for several years, but the betrayal of her
efforts by his telling her son that she was having an affair taxed the
relationship beyond its resource limits.  The resulting damage to
trust in the relationship fueled the woman's rage and made it easy
for her to encompass the entire marriage as being one betrayal
after another.  Her responses to the man's efforts to express love
toward her were consistent with her belief that he had damaged the
relationship beyond repair and that he was unwilling to change.

In the subsequent sessions as the man's efforts were directed
toward the grandchildren, the woman was willing to take a second
look at his loving efforts.  Not only was she willing to watch his
efforts, she actively joined him by helping him access memories
that might be meaningful to their lineage.  This shifted the
relational field of the couple from a feeling of despair to one of
hope.  Indeed, her suggestion that they go through old letters
together suggested that all relational resources from their marriage had not been wiped away, but that there was great hope that
the man could be trusted to express love.

The cotherapists suggested to the man that he consider writing
additional letters to the grandchildren, but that he make a special
effort in writing one of the female grandchildren.  The cotherapists
believed that the intense connection that the woman made with the

grandchildren around this effort would be most profound with the young girls of the family. In the next session, the man had written two letters. One was to a male grandchild recounting some boyhood stories about his relationship with his favorite dog. The other was a letter to one of the granddaughters who was age six. He had sent along a picture of his mother to the grandchild.

THERAPIST: Do you mind telling me some of what you said in the letter to your granddaughter?

MAN: No. I wrote her and told her about how I looked at this picture for a long time. I always remembered that my mother's hair was beautiful.

WOMAN: That is true. His mother had beautiful hair.

MAN: I told her that the color of her hair was the same as her great-grandmother's. I told her what a lovely little girl she was and how she would grow up and be beautiful. That was about it. I sent the picture along.

THERAPIST: What a wonderful gift to a 6-year-old. I can just imagine how that little girl must feel when she finds out that her granddaddy thinks she has beautiful hair. I bet she will think she is really special.

MAN: (*obviously touched with tears in his eyes*) I really hope so. She is very special.

WOMAN: (*after a long pause*) You know, [grandchild's name] has always been my favorite. I love them all, but I have always had a special connection with [grandchild's name]. I have been able to feel more with her. I think we are a lot alike. I've always thought she was the one who looked most like me. I think that letter really will be meaningful to her.

MAN: Well, she may have hair like my mother, but she is beautiful like you.

What started out as a half-hearted effort on the man's part to express care toward his grandchildren was now clearly becoming an important bonding agent between the husband and wife. As love was expressed to the grandchildren by recounting past experiences, the woman experienced the effort as evidence of trustworthy change. The connection that the woman made with the female grandchild was evident. When the man expressed to the woman before that he thought she was beautiful, the woman totally rejected his compliment. In the last session, however, his indirect compliment to her beauty through the grandchild was warmly welcomed and gladly accepted.

In doing the work of forgiving in the station of giving the opportunity for compensation, the therapist must help the victim mark progress on the victimizer's part in reestablishing trust and love. The points of demarcation give the victim a reference point to recount the victimizer's effort when the latter makes a relational mistake or fails to always be trustworthy. At the end of the session, the cotherapists worked with the woman to consolidate in her mind the trustworthy effort on the man's part. This work is very important if the victim is to make consistent and realistic progress toward releasing shame and anger and forgive the relational culprit who caused past damage and pain.

THERAPIST: Do you think that writing these things will do
           your husband good?
WOMAN:    Oh, yes. I think that this kind of connection is
           pleasurable for him. It brings him pleasure and
           connects him up—brings emotions to him. He
           worked hard at it. He worked almost a whole
           day typing the letter. It was good. It wasn't just
           doing nothing. I don't think he even realized
           how much it was actually doing.
           So he is doing something. I'm okay. I have felt
           a difference in him. For one thing, it's like a lot
           of anger has gone out of him. His face looks

different.  I'm a very sensitive person and I can
tell when there is a different feel to things.
Things feel different in the house.  When the
anger is gone, I can really feel it.
Even his color is different.  His face had a color
of anger and now it's gone.  It's not hard set
anymore.  He has changed.  He is different.  And
I hope it stays.
*(after a pause, she laughs)*  Our big argument
before was that I couldn't go to the kitchen
anytime without him intruding on my time.
Well, I've had to go in there and wake him up
sometimes when I want company.  Things are
different and it's better.

The dramatic shift in the status of trust in the relationship had
convinced the woman that the man had indeed changed.  This was
in direct opposition to her earlier raging declarations that he was
incapable of any change.  As the man lovingly reached out to the
grandchildren, he proved by his effort that he was somewhat
trustworthy.  In this light of the current responsible relational
giving, the past damage and hurt caused by his relational irresponsibility faded.

Although clear relational progress had been made in restoring
the relationship through the station of giving the opportunity for
compensation, much work in the process of forgiving remained.
The couple was still experiencing trustworthy actions that were
once removed from their relationship together.  As such, the real
tests of forgiving and forging a direct intimacy between the two
remained to be negotiated.  As the trust resources in the relationship were expanded and nurtured by the couple in their efforts
toward the grandchildren, the cotherapists once again moved the
man and woman to the point of addressing direct interactions
requiring love and trust.  As expected, this once again resurfaced
much of the pain and anger the couple experienced originally.

However, with the resources that were established in giving to the grandchildren, the woman was willing to accept the man's effort toward direct giving and could be helped to keep realistic expectations about their relationship.

Therapy with the couple oscillated between progress and regression for 20 more sessions. But in a very slow and calculated process, enough trust had been restored in the relationship that the marriage was stabilized. The work of forgiveness in the station of giving the opportunity for compensation is usually this type of long-term process. Although the process is usually difficult, the effort is well worth the prize if it yields relational stability or restoration.

*Chapter Ten*

# CLINICAL
# APPLICATION OF THE
# OVERT ACT OF
# FORGIVING

For many of us who grew up in the space age, there has always been a magical dream of spaceflight. When I was a young boy, my brothers and I were fascinated (and a little afraid) when Yuri Gargarin became the first man to orbit the earth. We were thrilled when Alan Shepard made his suborbital flight, becoming the first American in space, and were absolutely elated when John Glenn made his three orbits around the earth. When John Kennedy challenged the United States to land a man on the moon and bring him back safely by the end of the decade, I was convinced I had my life's calling. I was going to be an astronaut, and I was going to the moon!

Whatever fantasy and hope (after all, some *regular* people had flown on the space shuttle) remained with me about spaceflight ended dramatically on January 27, 1986. On that fateful day, the space shuttle *Challenger* was blown to pieces a little over two minutes after liftoff. An instant before, *Challenger* was flying high on what appeared to be a flawless launch, and then bang— all that remained were two wildly gyrating solid rocket boosters twisting around an enormous cloud of smoke. Seven astronauts, six of whom were like my boyhood heroes and one who was a regular person, were killed. Suddenly and tragically they were gone. There were no more illusions for me. Spaceflight may be glamorous when you are 7 years old, but risk and danger seem to have a special way of separating those of us who dream of the stars from those who have the right stuff to travel to them.

Many of us have a flashbulb memory of the *Challenger* exploding. As I sat for hours contemplating the image, I seemed to hope beyond hope that by some miracle, one of the astronauts would survive. Maybe they could have bailed out? No, the *Columbia* was the only shuttle that was ever equipped with an ejection system and that was only on the first two test flights. Maybe the *Challenger* detached from the external fuel tank and glided down? No, even under planned circumstances a glide landing is difficult. It took Sam Donaldson, who was reporting from the White House on the explosion, to shock me into reality. After being asked by Peter Jennings if the White House had any news about the astronauts, Donaldson responded, "You saw the explosion, there is no hope that anyone survived." His harsh words shocked my senses, but it was something I already knew. The shuttle was gone and the lives of seven people with it.

This is the kind of shock you feel when something unfair and damaging has taken place in your family. Families are supposed to be havens, where you can go when nothing else is working out. I suppose all of us, even when we realize that families are not perfect, have a "fantasy family" where members are always warm, always caring, and always nurturing. This fantasy is what we run into when someone viciously or insidiously damages a family member. The hurt and the pain are clearly evident to everyone including the victim. But somehow everyone, including the victim, wants to believe that the incident never happened or hopes that the consequences of the action will not damage anybody. Maybe if we sit and stare long enough, the reality of the injustice will not sink in or hurt will somehow be extracted.

Although there is little doubt that family damage can be so severe that there is no hope for salvage or restoration, most families are not *Challenger* disasters. Most families have the potential of the phoenix to rise from the ashes and disasters of the destructive past. They have a potential for true rebirth and restoration after destruction or damage. The fourth station of forgiveness, *the overt act of forgiving*, is not a practice of minimizing damage or reframing intentions of the family. In this station, the complete dimensions of the family injustices and the full impact of the resulting pain are laid bare for both the victim and the victimizer to view. In the reality of this tragic and shocking scene, the victim and victimizer move to reunite their relationship and responsibly promise each other trust and care to avoid future family debacles. Some of these relational miracles, especially when there are hideous family injustices, are no less amazing than if the *Challenger* had somehow emerged from the explosion intact and safe.

## THE THERAPEUTIC CHALLENGE OF THE OVERT ACT OF FORGIVING

When a victim and victimizer face one another for the express purpose of facing the painful past, there is tremendous energy in the room. It is a special kind of family volatility that can move either way: to a new constructive relationship of trust and love or to a defensive and potentially destructive contest that inflicts further damage on both victim and victimizer. Therefore, I believe that it is absolutely essential for the therapist working with families with a destructive past to do everything possible to keep the work constructive. In the work of forgiveness, individuals come to trust the therapist that the risky work of confronting the family past can be beneficial. Although the therapist cannot guarantee that the risk of opening up oneself to a painful family relationship will be healing, there must be a conscious effort on the therapist's part to try to make sure that the risk taken by the victim will not result in making his or her life worse. This determination by the therapist to keep the constructive potential of the relationship on track is applicable not only to the victim but also to the victimizer. The therapist has a responsibility to the victimizer to ensure that therapy does not end up as a blaming or persecution session in which the victimizer is put through a horrible inquisition.

In order to minimize this destructive potential in the overt act of forgiving, the therapist can keep the effort constructive in three ways. First, it is very important for the overt act of forgiveness to take place in therapy with the therapist present. Certainly overt forgiveness takes place between people outside of therapy. But when a person or family with a damaged past has come to therapy for help, the most powerful and dangerous step taken will be in the overt act of forgiving. It indeed seems irresponsible to work with individuals or families to help them in the process of forgiving and then send them off to face the difficult task of setting the past right by themselves. No matter how clear the therapist's instructions and how many times a therapist role-plays a critical confrontation with a victim, there is little substitute for the therapist's actually being there to mediate and coach the process. The therapist should be an objective buffer between the victim and the victimizer who has the interests of both at heart and has the skills and tools necessary to protect both. Leaving the victim and the victimizer alone to do this overt work greatly multiplies the risk potential. Many times the therapist must be willing to make sacrifices to be present with both the victim and the victimizer. It may require weekend sessions, extended half-day or full-day sessions, therapy outside the office, or even travel with the client back to a location. In most cases in which the victim wants to pursue this overt act of forgiving as a way of healing the past, however, the sacrifices by the therapist will pay therapeutic dividends.

Second, the therapist must be able to be partial to both the victim and the victimizer. Many times a client who comes from a damaged past will be the only one to come to therapy. In these instances, the therapist is usually privy to only one side of the family story and may become extremely biased. It is essential that the therapist maintain a position where he or she can know and understand the victim and the victimizer. In this way, the therapist is able to protect and be responsible to both members of the family in a caring and trustworthy manner. Without this perspective, the therapist may be put into the position where the victim always expects support in accusations against the "evil" victimizer, or where the victimizer sees the therapist as the "mastermind" behind the uninformed and nonunderstanding effort to attack him or her. Again, the contextual therapy technique of multidirected partiality (Boszormenyi-Nagy & Krasner, 1986) is most helpful in maintaining a position of advocate for both victim and victimizer, which in turn helps the therapist in the effort to mediate between the two. In order to be partial to the interests of both victim and victimizer, however, the therapist must spend time with both. If the therapist has never seen the alleged victimizer of the family, it is difficult and usually unwise to proceed with the work of the overt act of forgiving until there has been ample opportunity to hear the story of the victimizer.

Finally, the therapist's willingness to coach and be directive in the overt act of forgiving will assist the family in keeping the effort constructive. In this station in the work of forgiveness, the family members are gathered for what *they expect* to be a watershed event in their lives together. The event feels forced and prescribed because it is manipulated to happen in just such a fashion. It is much like a wedding, funeral, or other type of ceremony where there has been a gathering for a specific purpose. Imagine how difficult it would be if you showed up for a wedding and there was no direction from anyone on how to carry off the affair. When and how would the couple be married? Would the bride and groom automatically assume they were married if there was no direction? The fact is that when we change direction in life, it helps if we have lines of demarcation that direct us and delineate for us the change. The therapist is in the position to give direction in the overt act of forgiving. There are many ways to direct this process. Some therapists direct by taking a parental role, some by supportive coaching, some by demonstration, and some by subtle and friendly suggestion. Some therapists will use combinations of many different roles in giving direction in the work of forgiveness. But without the therapist's willingness to guide the process in the overt act of forgiving, anxiety in meetings between family members will increase and the opportunity for destructive behaviors will multiply.

## CASE EXAMPLE: SOMEONE HAS GOT TO TAKE RESPONSIBILITY

In the following case example, a 39-year-old woman who stated she was depressed came to therapy. When asked about her depressed feelings, she said that she felt bad because of "the awful things she had done in the past." The woman had been married for 15 years and had a 9-year-old son and a 7-year-old daughter. The woman worked as a secretary for a manufacturing firm and was an extremely responsible and hardworking employee. Although she described her marriage as not being particularly happy, she was quick to state that the relationship was manageable and "not in any trouble." It was obvious in the initial session that the woman had an alternating mix of anger and shame connected with her past.

THERAPIST: Tell me a little about the family you come from.
WOMAN: (*in a somewhat harsh tone*) It was okay. My parents seem to manage okay. I'm not exactly sure what you are looking for.
THERAPIST: I'm not sure that I am looking for anything except that I want to understand a little about you. I ask about your past because that is part of you.
WOMAN: (*remaining in the harsh tone*) I don't like to think about the past too much. There is a lot I don't

remember. I will say this, though, I had to make my way on my own. I didn't have help from my family. I was on my own.

THERAPIST: Your family, were they unfair to you?

WOMAN: *(shrugs shoulders)* I don't know. There are things I don't like to think about. Some things shouldn't have happened the way they did, but I just moved past them.

THERAPIST: You have moved past them to have your own family and make a life for yourself. What kind of life do you have?

WOMAN: *(pause, and then very somberly)* I'm not happy. Some things I have done okay, but I think I may have done some terrible things.

THERAPIST: What kind of things?

WOMAN: *(after a long pause)* I can't tell you. I want to be able to but I can't get the words out. You will think I'm awful. I'm not really sure they happened.

THERAPIST: I can promise you that I won't think you are awful, but what do you mean you're not sure they happened?

WOMAN: *(after a pause)* I have been remembering some things in flashes. I just get a picture in my mind or a feeling of something about the past. I can't remember all of it—just part. It feels awful. I don't know what to do.

The therapist continued to reassure her that he would not reject her for things she had done in the past, but did not press her any further to tell him about the specifics. The woman did give a few specifics about her family of origin in the session: She came from a large family with six children. Both of her parents were living, and she had two older sisters and one older brother, and one younger sister and brother. The family members had lived in the same area all their lives. Her hesitancy to tell the therapist any specifics about the past or the flash memories she was having was interpreted as her hesitancy to trust the therapist with the information. This is not unusual with people who come from abusive or damaging families. In such cases, therapists are well-advised to reassure clients, but not to push them into trusting a situation before they are ready. In this case, the therapist was cautious in continuing to ask questions about the past, and did not press the woman to answer with specifics. At the end of the second session, the woman started to trust the therapist enough to reveal a small part of her distress.

WOMAN:      (*with long pauses between statements*) I get so angry so quickly. I get afraid that I'm going to do something to one of my kids.

THERAPIST: Have you ever done anything that would hurt them?

WOMAN:      No. I mean I've spanked them when they did something wrong but never hurt them. I never have been abusive.

THERAPIST: What would make you believe that you might be abusive to them now?

WOMAN:      (*pause, and then very softly*) I think that I have gotten so angry before that I've done some crazy things. I remember having a bat in my hand and being so mad that I smashed up a car.

THERAPIST: Do you remember whose car?

WOMAN:      (*nodding head*) I think so.

The woman went on to reveal that the car that she smashed with a bat belonged to an old boyfriend whom she had dated in the years before she married. Although she was not sure of the actual time of the incident, she was fairly confident that it was around the time they ended their relationship. In the next session, the therapist began to ask about the circumstances surrounding the relationship and how it ended. The woman recounted how she had become involved with the man and how she came to depend on him for "my self-worth." Evidently, she was overinvolved to the point that she had trouble functioning when she was away from him. She stated that she would have done anything for him but that he treated her very badly by being verbally, and at times physically, abusive. When the relationship ended, she felt devastated and would follow him when he was out. When she failed to get him to reconcile with her or pay any attention to her, she reported that she was filled with rage and retaliated by smashing his car.

When the therapist suggested that this was one incident, the woman suggested that "there were other times" her anger had gotten out of control. It was unclear if the woman's memory of these incidents was blocked or if she did not trust the therapist enough to reveal any more information at the time. The therapist ended the session by suggesting that maybe she was fearful of her anger coming out in her family because she had once felt just that type of anger in her family or that perhaps it reminded her of being treated badly in her family. At the beginning of the fourth session, the woman began to open up about memories and feelings concerning her family of origin.

WOMAN:    Some things that you said last week reminded me of some stuff that happened in my family.

THERAPIST: What part?

WOMAN:    When you said that I felt angry in my family like I did with my boyfriend.
(*very long pause*) One time. (*pause*) When I was about twelve. (*pause, then a heavy sigh*) My brother and a few boys trapped me in a shed behind our house. (*in a very soft voice*) We were back there playing. They were making all sorts of comments to me—I didn't think too much about it. Then they all came at me. They raped me. (*starts to cry*)

THERAPIST: *(after several minutes)*  They raped you.  How awful for you.  Your own brother?

WOMAN:    *(still crying)*  Yes.

THERAPIST: Was there anybody to protect you?

WOMAN:    *(after a very long pause)*  You have to understand.  In my family, there was no one to tell.  *(again, after a very long pause)*  My daddy drank too much.  As long as I could remember, he was always hitting on me.  I would try and stay away from him, but when he would be drinking he would get out of control.
*(pause)*  I would know that he was going to do something bad to somebody—one of the girls.  I sometimes could joke around with him and get him to stop.  *(pause)*  Sometimes though he would take me out in his car and go out where I couldn't be heard.  He would start trying to kiss me and fondle me.

THERAPIST: *(after several minutes)*  Did he rape you too?

WOMAN:    No.  I was always able to fight him off.
*(long pause, then starts to cry heavily)*  I remember one time that he came home drunk with one of his friends.  Me and my younger sister were the only ones there at the house.  I sent my sister into the field and I hid under the bed.  *(pause)*  Daddy and that man were going through the house looking for me—saying what they would do when they found me.
*(pause)*  I can still smell that smell like it was under the bed.  I was so afraid!

THERAPIST: Did they find you?

WOMAN:    No.  They finally left.  *(pause, cries again)*  I was so scared.

THERAPIST: Are these some of the things you have been remembering that you have talked about?  *(the woman nods her head)*  So your brother and his

|  | friends did the same thing that your father was doing to you. *(woman nods again and cries)* *(after a pause)* You have told me many times that you have done awful things. It sounds to me that awful things have been done to you. |
| --- | --- |

WOMAN:    *(still crying)* I've always felt things like this were my fault. I have always been called a spitfire in my family. I have been the tough one. I've been cocky. I think they thought I could handle it—I don't know. Maybe they thought I deserved it.

THERAPIST: Have you felt like you deserved it?

WOMAN:    Sometimes.

The woman's response indicated the internalized shame she felt for the horrible sexual abuse she experienced and also made sense of the externalized anger she exhibited. She was used in the worst way in her family. When the therapist questioned the woman about her mother's and older sisters' knowledge of the abuse, she gave ambivalent answers indicating that they probably were aware of the sexual abuse but had the same fears she did. The rest of the session was spent in the therapist's identifying with and comforting the woman for the unjust abuse she experienced and shifting responsibility to the father, brother, and others who were abusive to her.

In the next session, the woman revealed a legacy of additional abuse from her family of origin, as well as other relationships. She reported that during the last week she had had alternating periods of depression and anger. In the session, she was extremely active to the point of fidgeting as she would recall certain events and then move as if to get the thought or the memory out of her mind. In the seventh session, the therapist moved to establish the responsibility for the sexual abuse with the father and brother. When he would talk about the abusive father, the woman's intensity and anger would subside.

THERAPIST: When we talk about your brother, you are
enraged at him.  But when we talk about your
daddy, you seem to not be as mad.

WOMAN: My brother is no good.  But I just can't feel that
way about my daddy.

THERAPIST: I can understand part of that.  Your father is
much more important than your brother.  But at
the same time, your daddy sexually abused you.
Your brother may have even gotten the idea in
his head to rape you from your daddy.

WOMAN: I know, but it's hard.  Daddy is old now.  He and
Mama are okay.  I just can't stand to go by and
see them and think about those things that happened.

THERAPIST: *(after a pause)*  So you can't put the responsibility on him for the sexual abuse, so maybe you put
it all on your brother.
*(pause)*  Or maybe you take the responsibility
yourself and just say you are a "bad" person.

WOMAN: Maybe.  Someone has got to take the responsibility.  It might as well be me.

THERAPIST: But when you take it and it actually belongs to
him, it seeps out of you and catches you off
guard.  It gets you in your memories.  It gets you
when you get angry at your kids.  It gets you
when you feel depressed.  When you make
yourself responsible for your father's actions, you
have to believe something about yourself that
isn't true.  You have to believe that you somehow
deserved it.  I want you to know, that I know that
you didn't deserve what happened to you.  You
are not bad, they were wrong.

The woman listened carefully to the therapist and became very
contemplative at this point in the session.  It appeared that the
connection of the responsibility for the abuse with her shame and

anger made sense to her. In the next session, she returned to therapy in a quite different state of mind. She stated that "finally for the first time in my life I don't think I'm a bad person." She began to speak with a marked amount of anger about how she should have never put up with her father's abuse and should have "thrown a fit" in the family until something was different. Clearly, the shift of responsibility had empowered the woman.

The new energy the woman had discovered from the insight led her to want to "get things right in the family." As the therapist started working with the woman on different ways to gain insight or understanding, or even on giving the opportunity for compensation, she would move the discussion back to "getting things right" with her father. There was good reason to believe in the case that the sisters of the family and the mother had also been abused. Confronting the brother who raped her might have been safer because she had little or no apparent emotional tie to him. But the woman had little interest in learning more about the family, understanding the abuse, or even how to prevent such abuse from ever occurring again. She was resolute in her belief that she could not move on until she had confronted her father. The therapist was able to constrain her from leaving the session and confronting the father that day by saying that she might have a chance for things to work out better if she confronted her father in a session with the therapist present.

There are many times when therapists see an opportunity where the overt act of forgiveness will benefit an individual and family and they may therapeutically move the family to that end. At other times, the individual or family will make it clear that any salvage or restoration in the family is dependent upon an overt confrontation of the unjustified damage. In these instances, the risk is great because the family is put into a critical "one shot" session or sessions to work things out. It is clear, however, that when an individual or family feels this type of need to proceed, the work of exonerating and forgiving cannot be achieved unless the session is tried. In such cases, it is wise for the therapist to support the effort and move to coach the individual or family on how to best use the confrontation as an opportunity for restoration.

It is important for the therapist to know when the client is wanting a confrontation for the purpose of a "rage session" against the victimizer and when the client is really interested in restoration. Rage and blame may come out in any session, but if it is the intent of the meeting, then it is clearly not the work of forgiveness. In this case, the therapist was confident that the woman cared for her father because of her continued care for him and her mother. She was willing to work with the therapist for two sessions so they could discuss the best way to meet with the father with the optimal chance of setting the transgression right.

In the next two sessions, the therapist role-played with the woman different scenarios of conversations, different possible responses of the father were explored, and decisions were made on where to meet and whom to involve in the session. After the second session of preparation, the woman told her father that she had been going to therapy for several weeks because she had been depressed. She stated that she could use his help in getting over her depression and asked if he would come to the next session. When the father asked if the mother was coming, she said that she wanted to work with him first and maybe the mother could help later. The father agreed to come to the next session.

Two hours were planned for the session, even though the afternoon was cleared if it was needed. The therapist spent the first half hour joining with and talking to the father with the daughter present in the room. The father was a retired carpenter who also raised some grain and a few farm animals on a small acreage farm. Although he spoke fondly of his daughter, he was unclear about many of the details about his children's lives. When the therapist asked about how family life was for him when the children were growing, he stated that he "drank too much back then and it made life miserable for everyone." He also said that he no longer drank because of health reasons, and the daughter agreed that he no longer drank.

THERAPIST: *(to the father)* Your daughter came to me saying that she was depressed and feeling bad about some things she had remembered. I asked you to come here so you could help shed some light on the things that upset her when she can't remember all the details.

FATHER: [Woman's name] has always been strong. She has always pulled her own weight and has sure taken care of me and her mother. I'll do anything that I can.

*(Therapist motions to the woman to proceed.)*

WOMAN: I've remembered some things that hurt awful bad. *(pause)* I remember that sometimes when you drank... I remember some things happening that were not too good.

FATHER: *(somber and staring at the floor)* I know there were a lot of things that were wrong when I drank. I know that I would make things hard when I drank. But I don't think I drank too much. I always tried to provide for you kids.

WOMAN: I remember that you drank a lot.

At this point, the therapist blocked the interaction between the daughter and the father because it would be unproductive in the end. The father interpreted his daughter's initial statement as an accusation and moved to defend his parenting while acknowledging that he drank some. The daughter was quick to respond defensively, wanting to clarify that the father drank heavily. Although it may have been an issue for a later time, the issue at the present was not the father's drinking, but the "bad things" that happened when he drank. The therapist assured the father that he knew that the father cared for his daughter by his willingness to come and then redirected the daughter to discuss the "bad things."

WOMAN: I keep having a memory. When I was 11, I remember you came home drunk with [man's

name].  Me and [sister's name] were the only
ones home.  You started saying that you were
going to take me... you were going to take me to
bed with you.  You told [man's name] he could
take [sister's name].  *(starts to cry)*

FATHER:      When was this?

WOMAN:       It happened when I was about eleven.

FATHER:      I don't remember that ever happening.

THERAPIST:   Sometimes things happen and you can't remember.  Especially when you have had too much to
drink.  The important thing is not the memory,
but how the memory made her feel.
How do you think it would have made her feel if
her father would have said such a thing to a
friend?

FATHER:      *(after a pause, looks at his daughter who is now
staring down)*  Well, I would imagine that it
would have scared her to death.  Made her feel
like I didn't love her.

WOMAN:       I sent [sister's name] into the field and I hid
under the bed. Both of you started going through
the house saying what you were going to do.  I
was so scared.

FATHER:      *(after a pause)*  I swear that I don't remember.  If
I remembered something like that, I would tell
you.  I would own up to it.

THERAPIST:   Again, what is important is how the memory
makes her feel.  To an 11-year-old, to have your
drunk father seeking you out to have sex with
him would be terrifying.  Fathers are supposed to
protect.  I know that you don't remember, but I
guess I'm wondering where this memory comes
from.

FATHER:      I don't know. I don't think she would lie about
something like that.

THERAPIST:   Do you think that the situation could have hap-

FATHER:          pened like that, even if you don't remember it?
                 (*after a long pause*) I don't remember it, but
                 something like that could have happened. There
                 are a lot of things I don't remember when I was
                 drinking.

It is likely that the father actually did not remember the incident that his daughter was describing. However, the therapist moved the father to identify with the daughter's feelings as if he did remember the situation. His statement acknowledging that something that terrible could have happened when he was drinking linked the daughter and father in at least partial *agreement* about the past violation. While the specifics were not delineated, the father's belief that such a violation of love and trust could have indeed occurred encouraged the daughter to go on with her description of past memories.

WOMAN:           There were a lot of times when I started getting
                 older that you would come home after drinking
                 some. (*pause*) You would say you were feeling
                 "frisky," and you would pinch us and poke us.
FATHER:          I was always teasing with you girls. Especially
                 you. I probably shouldn't have done it.
THERAPIST:       (*to the woman*) Where did he pinch you and
                 poke you? Show him.

At this point the therapist intervened to prevent the father from reframing the intent to abuse as a loving tease. By asking the woman to show where she was "pinched," he brought the inappropriate and irresponsible behavior into the present in a powerful way. After hesitating, the woman pointed to the areas the father fondled and teased. After staring at the floor a few minutes, the father continued.

FATHER:          I have done some things that I am ashamed of. I
                 didn't treat you girls like I should have. When I

drank, I did some bad things and I know I did. But I did care for all of you.

WOMAN:     I remember that you use to take me out and try to kiss me and take my shirt off. I remember having to fight you.

FATHER:     *(after a long pause)* I know. I can remember something like that happening. I drank and I did some awful things.

WOMAN:     You remember taking me out in your car?
            *(father nods head in acknowledgment)*

FATHER:     That's an awful thing for a father to admit. I'm sorry it ever happened. I'd do anything to be able to set the time back.

Here the father clearly acknowledged his responsibility for the violation. Instead of a vague memory, he at least had a partial memory of taking the woman out and sexually abusing her. At this point in the session, the woman was clearly validated for part of the hideous sexual abuse she suffered that drained trustworthiness from the family. It seemed that she was almost taken off guard by the father's acknowledgment. For the next several minutes, the woman tried to recount specific incidents with the father that she had remembered to get his acknowledgment and explanation. The father had only vague recollections of specifics and varied his explanations between apology and drinking too much. The therapist finally blocked the daughter's questioning to focus the session on potential reconciliation.

THERAPIST:  *(to the father)* You said a little while ago that you would do anything to turn back time. If you could turn back time and your daughter was eleven...and if you had been out drinking too much...*(pause)* and if you came home feeling frisky...*(pause)* and if you were feeling like you were getting close to sexually abusing her, what do you wish would have happened?

FATHER:      *(long pause)* I wish I would have gone to sleep it off. I wish I would have never drank in the first place. It caused a lot of pain. I sure wish I never would have hurt you *(looking at the daughter).* *(daughter looks down and starts to cry)*

THERAPIST: *(after a pause)*   And if you could turn back time and your daughter was still eleven, but you had already abused her, what do you wish you would have done then?

FATHER:      *(long pause)* I should have gotten help. I should have done anything I could to make sure that it would never happen again. I remember promising to myself that it would never happen again. I should have gone to get some help instead of waiting.

THERAPIST: Well, what has happened has happened. There is no way to turn back the clock. But the promise you made to yourself then, you never made to anyone else. Your daughter is still here even though this happened many years ago. Maybe you could talk to her now.

The father turned to the daughter and once again said that he was sorry. He stated very clearly that if he had it to do over again, he would seek help in order to protect her and stop his drinking. In this last interchange, the father clearly apologized to the daughter and in essence promised that it would never happen again. Even though the father was long past sexually abusing the daughter, the promise of change was still essential to the daughter to ensure that there had been a change in the status of love and trust between the two. The issue of carrying the responsibility for the sexual abuse was claimed by the father, and the daughter was relieved of its weight.

Much of the rest of the session was spent discussing the ramifications for the family of such a disclosure. The father stated repeatedly that he was ready to come clean with the entire family.

The woman, however, was much more hesitant about discussing the abuse with any other family members. This hesitancy may have been for several reasons. It is possible that the daughter wanted to protect her mother from the knowledge or did not trust her mother to handle the information in a responsible manner. It is also very likely that even though the woman wanted to make things right with her father, she was not ready to confront or try to reconcile with the brother who led a gang rape of her. The therapist suggested that the father and woman perform a ritual of burying a "token of promise" that the sexual abuse should never have happened and that it would never happen again. This promise would be secret between them until they both decided to share it with someone else, at which time they could dig up the token and share the promise. The father chose an old family picture out of his wallet, and the father and woman left to perform the ritual.

The woman continued to work with the therapist for another ten sessions. She eventually started attending a sexual abuse survivors group and continued to confront her painful abusive past. She and the father eventually shared the promise with the oldest sister, who was also dealing with sexual abuse, but did not choose to tell the mother or confront the brother. Still, the effect of the session on the woman was powerful. Her depression almost completely subsided, with the exception of a few bad days. Her confidence and self-esteem greatly increased, and she began to make specific efforts to improve her relationship with her husband. Most important to her, her unspecified rage and overreaction to frustrating situations and her children subsided greatly. Certainly the overt act of forgiving in this case did not automatically make a very dysfunctional family healthy, but it did provide a new beginning of love and trust between the woman and the father. This reestablished trust provided a resource for the woman and set her on the track of living more successfully and hopefully of continuing to heal herself.

*Section Three*

# Issues and Questions in the Work of Forgiveness

*Chapter Eleven*

# QUESTIONS CONCERNING THE WORK OF FORGIVENESS

A s I mentioned in the Preface, this book is not intended to be the whole story on the work of forgiveness. Forgiveness is extremely complex and happens differently for different people in various situations. What this book has tried to accomplish, however, is to provide *one* therapeutic framework to help therapists and individuals who work with, come from, or who are in families where there is severe injustice negotiate the difficult pathway of forgiveness. The four stations of forgiveness are conceptual frames to help therapists and their clients find their way along the road, but it is the individuals in relationships who accomplish the actual work. Therefore, people may take different paths in their quest towards forgiveness of family members. However, I believe that this framework does provide a guide on how to maintain individual integrity and protection while seeking to connect with the family resources of love and trust that will make a person stronger and enable him or her to pass along these resources to other relationships.

Specifically, there are several areas of forgiveness that I have not touched on in this framework that people often question. The following are some of the more common questions that I have received.

*Q: There is a saying that goes "forgive and forget." Does*
*forgiving mean that you forget?*

Lewis Smedes (1984) correctly points out that forgiving and forgetting are two separate issues that are not connected by necessity. He points out that we seldom forget the action that damaged us in an unfair way, but we do tend to forget the pain that is associated with that action after we have forgiven. I believe this is true. Pain tends to fade with time after the work of forgiveness is achieved. When a person engages in the second two stations of forgiving and restores the relationship with a former relational culprit, then the pain of the past has the opportunity to fade when compared to the trustworthy and loving relationship of the present. The popular belief that if a person really forgives another, he or she will wipe the slate clean of all memories of the incident is simply not true. Even if it were neurologically possible on request to erase specific memory pathways in the brain that contain the information about the damaged past, it would not necessarily be preferable.

Again, at the heart of family injustice and pain is the violation of trust. If I am damaged by a family member, there is a sequential deterioration of trust. If I forgive and forget, then possibly nothing will change in a relationship with an untrustworthy family member, and I will open myself up to the same type of relational damage to occur again. The station of insight requires that changes in the transactional patterns in the family occur to prevent further relational deterioration. If I try to forget the damage, then I will not remember the necessary steps to take to prevent such damage in the future and there is a possibility that I will be "twice burned."

Trust is best restored to a relationship not when the victim and victimizer act as if no violation ever occurred; it works best when they do not forget the past and choose to live life differently.

> *Q: How does one go about the work of forgiving when a family member, like a mother or a father, who has caused damage has died?*

The work of forgiveness as I have outlined includes both exonerating and forgiving. Exoneration is just as much a part of the work of forgiveness as the effort put forth to restore a damaged relationship. Exonerating a family member who has caused us great harm means removing the load of culpability from the person by the station of understanding and preventing the damage from ever harming us or our posterity again through the station of insight. In short, exonerating salvages the family resources for ourselves and the intergenerational lineage. Forgiving, however, is the reconstruction of the relationship. Trust and love are rebuilt because the opportunity (and risk) is presented to both the victim and the victimizer to interact differently in a nondestructive manner.

As I conceptualize the work of forgiveness, exonerating a dead or unavailable family member who caused us unjustified harm is quite possible and can bring a victim a great amount of peace. However, the work of forgiveness requires access back to the relationship itself. Therefore, forgiving as in the last two stations of giving the opportunity for compensation or the overt act of forgiving, is not possible. Donald Williamson (1991) provides excellent direction using preparation and ritual in negotiating the difficult task of making final resolution of issues with a parent who has died.

> *Q: Are there situations where family damage is so severe that forgiveness is not appropriate?*

I fear that the answer is yes. It causes fear in me because I believe that the consequences for a victim who comes from such a family are terrible indeed. Although human beings have a remarkable capability to love and nurture one another, I do believe that there are a few so powerful in their destructive capabilities that most of us are not wise enough to master enough insight to stop them. In these situations, there is little we can do but to isolate from the destructive capability. It is much like the land surrounding the Chernobyl nuclear reactor site in the former Soviet Union. The nuclear core is still highly active and quite dangerous. Much damage has been done, but there is little that can be done now to reverse the destruction. All that one can do is pull back from the site and watch as the awful effects of the lethal radiation play out in the lives of the population and the country.

Individuals who come from such destructive situations can certainly move on, be nurtured by friends and other institutions, and nurture others in a trustworthy manner. The people that I have seen do this successfully carefully monitor their behavior and gauge their actions to make sure they are not passing along past damage to others or believing shameful messages they were given by a victimizer. But even with the people I know who have successfully overcome destructive families without the work of forgiveness, there are lingering effects that cause them pain from time to time. Unfortunately, however, many continue to be destructive to themselves and others in many ways.

*Q: Can victims actually forgive a person who has violated them in a severe way if the relational culprit never owns up to the responsibility or refuses to apologize?*

For many people who have been damaged and violated in their families, nothing less than a full recognition and responsible accounting by the victimizer will do. This is a difficult position for all concerned. The victim usually desires an acknowledgment and apology from the victimizer as a verification of the victim's damage and rights to vindication. Many times, however, victimizers have been victims themselves and will see their actions as being justified in light of the violations they have experienced. I see this occur often in therapy when adult children will demand that abusive parents take responsibility for some abusive actions in the past and the parents will defend themselves as "good" parents. In fact, from the parents' perspective of past violation, they feel justified in having parented the best they knew how. In reality, although parents may be abusive, I have found that many times they were much better parents than their own parents were for them.

Victims do hold a claim to the pain and violation that they feel. However, if all that will suit the victim is for the victimizer to acknowledge the irresponsibility and appropriately apologize, there is a high likelihood that the damaged victimizer will refuse. This will leave both the victim and the victimizer completely frustrated in the work of forgiving. However, there is much of the work of forgiveness that can be achieved through the three stations of insight, understanding, and giving the opportunity for compensation. This work is dependent upon the willingness of the victim to work through methods of forgiveness other than the overt act of forgiving.

*Q: There are many who have been severely abused by their families who believe that you should never forgive because the violator can never be trusted. What do you say to this belief?*

Certainly a person's decision to perform the hard work of forgiveness is highly personal, and each situation is different. I would never, for instance, tell clients that they must forgive someone who victimized them for any reason. Individuals who have been a victim of abuse must make their own decision on how best to handle family relationships.

However, I believe that most of the people who have been abused in some way by a family member make this statement about forgiveness because they see that the anger they feel toward the violator fuels energy that drives them to achieve a higher sense of personal regard and protection against future abuse. I am in agreement that victims of unjustified harm must be able to protect themselves from an untrustworthy family member. No one is benefited when victims forgive an untrustworthy person who will hurt them again. However, I conceptualize this ability to stop the damage as part of the process of forgiveness in the station of insight. I argue that it is part of forgiveness because no relationship has the chance of being restored to a loving and trustworthy potential if damage keeps on occurring. Learning how to protect oneself from future damage is the first step forward in salvage of the remaining relationship.

*Q: What if the victimizer is the one who wants to seek forgiveness for damage that he or she has caused in the family? Does the process work in the opposite direction?*

I believe that the answer is absolutely yes. The victimizer is in an excellent position to accomplish the work of forgiveness because initiation on the victimizer's part is usually an indication of responsible and trustworthy action. As such, the work of overt forgiveness or compensation through responsible giving can be much more intentional and direct.

There are times, however, when the victimizer's seeking forgiveness is potentially damaging. If the victimizer has asked for and received forgiveness many times in the past and has continued to be relationally irresponsible, the victim of the violation who is asked overtly to forgive is put in a difficult position of trusting in the face of past and continuing damage. In these cases, I find it helpful for the victimizer not to address the violation in a direct way with the victim. It is often much more helpful for the victimizer to compensate the victim through current responsible giving and *prove* his or her trustworthiness and care to the victim. This often gives the victim a new baseline of behavior to reference with regard to the victimizer and can eventually lead to a more overt forgiveness later.

Of course, a victimizer who wants to reconcile the past has no guarantee that a victim will be willing to forgive and restore the relationship. In these cases, it is still possible for the victimizer to pursue the work of forgiveness by the stations of insight and understanding. Insight helps the victimizer recognize actions that caused harm and can be changed, while understanding can help the victimizer identify and empathize with the victim who suffered the violation.

*Q: Many people who come from damaging families would like to work toward overt forgiveness, but doing so may release family secrets that other family members (such as siblings) do not want released. How can they deal with this situation?*

This situation is very common, especially in abusive families, and it works two ways. First, a person who was abused may want to confront the issue openly in the family while the family wants to keep the secret. In these cases, the person seeking to forgive may be victimized again as the family becomes emotionally and verbally abusive. Unfortunately, I have seen several instances where a well-meaning victim has been called a liar and essentially excommunicated from the family. The past is powerful and painful, and many times the pain is so great that other family members will join in a coalition against one of their own to keep the pain internalized. Of course, this is extremely destructive and works against the very love and trust that it is hoped will be achieved in the work of forgiveness. Again, the first three stations of forgiveness require no overt confrontation in the family. They often are a safer way to pursue forgiveness without risking further emotional damage. In many instances, victims will see this as a compromise of their claim on the damage. However, I often remind my clients that it is a long life and if the salvage and restoration effort is kept on track to a constructive end at the beginning of forgiveness, there are always other opportunities to pursue it overtly.

The other way this issue sometimes presents itself is in anger and resentment from siblings. Often in abusive families, adult siblings form a solid coalition against relationally irresponsible parents. If one of the siblings decides to pursue the work of forgiveness and is successful in restoring the relationship, the sibling coalition may be broken. This may result in fractured relationships as brothers and sisters cannot understand how their sibling could ever reconcile with the parent. The loyalty of the victim who is seeking to forgive is therefore split as to whether to restore a relationship with parents or maintain a coalition with siblings.

I find it helpful in these cases to ask the siblings who feel threatened by the forgiving victim to come to therapy so the feelings and issues can be discussed overtly. In this way, the siblings can often be made to understand that the love and trust between them is not dependent upon their being aligned against their parents. Often, siblings that were held together by a common pain or complaint against a parent are now in a position to develop a fuller and more complete relationship based solely on their affection and care for one another. Most of the time, once the siblings realize that the relationship will change but not end, the animosity will fade. However, there are instances where relationships between siblings are placed in jeopardy. The therapist and victim seeking to forgive are well advised to explore these various effects on family relationships so reactions and consequences do not come as a surprise to the victim.

*Q: How does one know when a person is really sorry for past family violations that he or she has "caused"?*

The truth is that there is no way to be absolutely sure of any person's motive in any type of interaction. We learn to trust people with whom we have relationships by the demonstration of their responsible giving and by their absence of efforts to intimidate or manipulate us. In short, the only way we can be reasonably assured of others' thoughts and motives toward ourselves is to judge whether their actions match up fairly consistently with their words.

This is a particular challenge in forgiving and restoring a damaged relationship. The fact that victimizers in the past have proved untrustworthy makes it difficult to trust their current words or actions—especially with regard to an apology made for past damage as in the fourth station, the overt act of forgiveness. Even in the station of giving the opportunity for compensation, victims cannot totally escape or protect themselves from risk.

The only way to know if a person who has been irresponsible and untrustworthy in the past will be loving and trustworthy in the present is to give them an opportunity to do so. However, I do find that most often the therapist and the victim are able to "feel" the emotional environment in the interaction between the victim and the victimizer. If there is some change in the relationship, which I believe there will be if there is a true apology, it can usually be picked up by the therapist and the victim in the emotional affect of the person who is making the apology and the interchange with the victim.

*Q: There are many times that victims block the memories of specific past violations, even though they know that unjust violations have occurred. Can they do work in the fourth station of the overt act of forgiveness?*

It is hardly unusual for people to block out many of the specifics associated with past trauma. I believe that it does not rule out the work in the fourth station and in many ways may actually make the work easier. Often, it is difficult enough for the victim and victimizer to sit face to face and talk about past violation and pain. When there is a vast memory of violation after violation, the victim may have the tendency to want to get acknowledgments of as many different situations as possible. This increases the likelihood that the victim and victimizer will have different memories of the event or that there will be defensiveness between the two if numerous incidents are revealed.

At the heart of the violation between the two is unjustified action that produced a judgment on the part of the victim with regard to the relational love and trust. In any overt act of forgiveness, the victim and victimizer must center on these feelings in the relational reality instead of the specifics of each event. Therefore, many times I will have the victim who has specific memories choose one that served as a watershed of evidence of this absence of love and trust. This makes identification, acknowledgment, and apology much easier as the victim and victimizer encapsulate the heart of the violation without addressing every detail of the relationship. With individuals who have blocked memories or have very few memories, this process of getting the victim and victimizer to deal with the emotional field of the relationship and identify with one another can be much easier.

It is very common in these situations after there is an overt act of forgiving between the victim and victimizer for either to have dramatic memories about past abuses that were not accessible before. These usually can be dealt with in a constructive way as both are willing to continue relating in a loving and trustworthy way. However, sometimes victims will have a memory of a violation so severe and terrible that they are filled with intense anger and shame, some of which they may have never felt before.

It is wise for the therapist to prepare the victim who has these memory blocks for the recalling of the painful past, especially if the overt act of forgiveness is successful. I have had much success in working with victims in this situation using cognitive techniques that remind them of the loving and trustworthy work done by the victimizer in the overt act of forgiveness even while they are in the midst of recalling a painful past memory.

It is essential that the therapist help the victim not lose the work of forgiveness already accomplished because of a backwash of pain from the past. If the therapist keeps reminding the victim of this perspective of the past in light of the current relationship with the victimizer, the pain usually subsides more quickly than the original work of forgiveness. Also, most victimizers are more willing to redress specific painful memories with members after they have experienced the overt act of forgiving. This gives the past victimizer another opportunity to demonstrate a trustworthy bond with the past victim and ensure him or her that the present relationship has indeed changed.

> *Q: Many people feel obligated to forgive others because of*
> *their religious beliefs. Does this framework work for or*
> *against a client's religious beliefs?*

Most of the people I work with who have trouble with this concept of forgiveness come from a Judeo-Christian framework. They look in the Old or New Testament and find specific instances where God commands people to forgive those who have "sinned" against them or who have done them evil. As many of these people will point out, the scripture says that if they do not forgive their "brother," then God will not forgive them.

It appears to me that many of the assumptions about the concept of religious forgiveness are pulled from scripture that is isolated from its context. Indeed, if we are to take the Old and New Testaments in their entire context, then they are stories about God's redemptive and restorative work for humankind as a whole. True, there are many instances like God's redeeming the Israelites and joining in relationship with them, as in their exodus out of Egypt. But God also makes it clear in the Old Testament that the fall of Jerusalem to Babylon is due to his judgment for Israel's unfaithful behavior. Taken in context with one another, both situations are intended by God to work eventual redemption. In the framework that I have outlined, the exodus from Egypt would be the two stations of giving the opportunity for compensation and the overt act of forgiving. The fall of Jerusalem and the Babylonian captivity would be the station of insight as God outlines to His people what he expects as trustworthy and appropriate behavior.

I believe you find the same types of examples throughout the New Testament. Jesus did marvelously redeeming work by forgiving humankind's sin at the point of the crucifixion. He instructed his disciples to forgive those who do them wrong "seven times seventy" times. Yet this is the same Jesus who made no bones about calling the Pharisees and Sadducees snakes and herding merchants out of the temple with a whip. I believe that the religious commands to forgive are not edicts to put ourselves in dangerous and untrustworthy situations, but imperatives to have the intent to reconcile with those who do us unjustified harm. But if we are to follow the Judeo-Christian example of forgiveness, I believe that the restoration and reconciliation of relationships will include confrontation and protection in a trustworthy and disciplined way as well as compassion and understanding.

## SOME FINAL THOUGHTS ON THE WORK OF FORGIVENESS

I find it a remarkable fact that human beings, with all of their diverse races, cultures, beliefs, and personalities, continue to survive. In ages past and continuing into the present, there always seems to have been one group of humans that is willing to sacrifice the lives or rights of others just because they can or because doing so is deemed by them to have some "good" purpose. Blacks were captured, tortured, and enslaved on ships with little room, food, water, clean air, and taken from their native Africa to live out generations under the enormous burden of abuse by whites in Western culture. Native Americans were stripped of their land, food source, culture, and dignity as the new Americans moved west fulfilling their belief in their manifest destiny. Many Palestinians feel entitled to kill Jews and vice versa because many members of each group believe the other is "bad" and has infringed on their rights. Religion hates religion, tribe hates tribe. Capitalists and Marxists, conservatives and liberals—they all hate each other and essentially believe that the world would be a better place if the others were gone, and sometimes take it on as their lifelong goal to achieve that end. With all the evidence and history of one people making war on another people, it is amazing that any people has endured. As Maya Angelou once said when I heard her speak at the 16th Annual Family Therapy Network Symposium about the survival of blacks in this country, "The thinker must think, how have we survived?" Indeed, how have we survived?

Coursing through the historical veins of this tragic lineage that would appear to result in the extinction of many cultures and perhaps the entire human race is an element that keeps peoples alive. Basic sacrifice and giving of nurturing and love from one person to another in the context of relationship build trust and hope that assure that continuance. Even in tragic extermination of human races and cultures, almost always the sacrifices of the many end with the survival of the ones. In turn, those ones live on for the many and the people survive.

Families are the smaller units of the larger peoples. They are tied together through their struggle and somehow muster the energy to nurture members with love and trust. In turn, this nurturing has remarkable resiliency against the ravages of personal and even global violations. Families have this wonderful resource, but not all families utilize the resource. Some are destructive and threaten the survival of their posterity. But even in these destructive families, the members are tied together with their pasts and their futures intertwined. It behooves us—even the most damaging of families—to work for as much salvage and restoration in the relationships as possible. For if we sever and retaliate against those family members who have violated our just entitlements of love and trust, we also participate in the killing off of our common heritage and the survival of the lineage. Active murder of a family relationship casts us adrift from who we are as humans. The work of forgiveness is not only to heal the individual and the present family but also to ensure the survival of our people.

The work of forgiveness, however, is sloppy and messy work. Issues of working out family love and trust continue for a lifetime, and then the lifetimes of the coming generations. We usually move back and forth between the four stations of insight, understanding, giving the opportunity for compensation, and the overt act of forgiving many times and with a myriad of relationships we call family. In short, this work of forgiveness is very inexact. Still,

I believe that any work of forgiveness that is undertaken by a family member is a trustworthy expression of faith and care to the intergenerational heritage and posterity of all people.  For this reason, all of us have an interest in families and forgiveness.  We are all here—all of us—because someone in our past has provided at least a part of that faith and care.

# REFERENCES

Augsburger, D. (1981). *Caring enough to forgive*. Ventura, CA: Reagal Books.

Boscolo, L., Cecchin, G., Hoffman, L., & Penn, P. (1987). *Milan systemic family therapy*. New York: Basic Books.

Boszormenyi-Nagy, I. (1986). Transgenerational solidarity: The expanding context of therapy and prevention. *American Journal of Family Therapy*, *14*, 195–212.

Boszormenyi-Nagy, I., & Krasner, B. (1980). Trust-based therapy: A contextual approach. *American Journal of Psychiatry*, *137*, 767–775.

Boszormenyi-Nagy, I., & Krasner, B. (1986). *Between give and take: A clinical guide to contextual therapy*. New York: Brunner/Mazel.

Boszormenyi-Nagy, I., & Spark, G. (1984). *Invisible loyalties*. New York: Brunner/Mazel.

Boszormenyi-Nagy, I., & Ulrich, D. N. (1981). Contextual family therapy. In A. S. Gurman & D. P. Kniskern (Eds.), *Handbook of family therapy* (pp. 159-186). New York: Brunner/Mazel.

Bowen, M. (1978). *Family therapy in clinical practice*. New York: Jason Aronson.

Buber, M. (1970). *I and thou*. New York: Charles Scribner's Sons.

Erikson, E. H. (1985). *The life cycle completed: A review*. New York: Norton & Company.

Hargrave, T. D., & Anderson, W. T. (1992). *Finishing well: Aging and reparation in the intergenerational family*. New York: Brunner/Mazel.

Imber-Black, E. (1988a). Idiosyncratic life cycle transitions and therapeutic rituals. In B. Carter & M. McGoldrick (Eds.), *The changing family life cycle: A framework for family therapy*. New York: Gardner Press.

Imber-Black, E. (1988b). Ritual themes in families and family therapy. In E. Imber-Black, J. Roberts, & R. Whiting (Eds.), *Rituals in families and family therapy* (pp. 47–83). New York: Norton and Company.

Kobak, R. R., & Waters, D. B. (1984). Family therapy as a rite of passage: Play's the thing. *Family Process, 23,* 89–100.

Levy, L. P., Joyce, P. A., & List, J. A. (1988). Reconciliations with parents as a treatment goal for adolescents in an acute care psychiatric hospital. *Social Work in Health Care, 31*(1), 1–21.

Madanes, C. (1991). *Sex, love and violence: Strategies for transformation*. New York: W.W. Norton.

McGoldrick, M., & Gerson, R. (1985). *Genograms in family assessment*. New York: Norton & Company.

Minuchin, S. (1974). *Families and family therapy*. Cambridge: Harvard University Press.

Morrison, J. K. (1981). The use of imagery techniques in family therapy. *American Journal of Family Therapy, 9,* 52–56.

Palazzoli, M. S., Boscolo, L., Cecchin, G., & Prata, G. (1978). *Paradox and counter-paradox*. Northvale, NJ: Jason Aronson.

Papp, P., Silverstein, O., & Carter, E. A. (1973). Family sculpting in preventive work with "well families." *Family Process, 12,* 197–212.

Patton, J. (1985). *Is human forgiveness possible?* Nashville: Ambingdon Press.

Pettle, S. (1992). Review of *Sex, love and violence. Journal of Family Therapy, 14*(1), 99–100.

Pingleton, J. P. (1989). The role and function of forgiveness in the psychotherapeutic process. *Journal of Psychology and Theology, 17*(1), 27–35.

Satir, V. (1967). *Conjoint family therapy.* Palo Alto, CA: Science and Behavior Books.

Schneider, J. P. (1989). Rebuilding the marriage during recovery from compulsive sexual behavior. *Family Relations, 38,* 288–294.

Sherman, R., & Fredman, N. (1986). *Handbook of structured techniques in marriage and family therapy.* New York: Brunner/Mazel.

Smedes, L. B. (1984). *Forgive and forget.* New York: Harper & Row.

Smith, S. L. (1991). *Making peace with your family.* New York: Plenum Press.

Smith, T. E. (1991). Lie to me no more: Believable stories and marital affairs. *Family Process, 30*(2), 215–225.

Todd, E. (1985). The value of forgiveness according to Jung. *Journal of Religion and Health, 24*(1), 39–48.

Vande Kemp, H. (1987). Relational ethics in the novels of Charles Williams. *Family Process, 26*(2), 283–294.

Whitaker, C. (1982). *From psyche to system, the evolving theory of Carl Whitaker* (J. Neil & D. Kniskern, Eds.). New York: Guilford Press.

Williamson, D. S. (1991). *The intimacy paradox: Personal authority in the family system.* New York: Guilford Press.

# INDEX